Emily Post's

wedding parties

Also from the Emily Post Institute

Emily Post's

wedding parties

Anna Post

Collins

An Imprint of HarperCollins*Publishers*

HarperCollins books may be purchased for educational, business, or sales
promotional use. For information please write: Special Markets Department,
HarperCollins Publishers, 10 East 53rd Street, New York, NY 10022.

First Edition

Cover photo: © Kate Connell / Getty Images

Illustrations © Chesley McLaren

Produced by Smallwood & Stewart, New York City

Designed by Alexis Siroc

Library of Congress has Cataloging-in-Publication Data
has been requested.

ISBN: 978-0-06-122801-8
ISBN-10: 0-06-122801-X

07 08 09 10 RRD 10 9 8 7 6 5 4 3 2 1

CONTENTS

For my friends and family,
whose beautiful stories fill these pages.

ACKNOWLEDGMENTS

This book never could have been completed without the help of so many people. I'd like to give a huge thanks to Royce Flippin whose versatility, experience, (patience!), and dedication were invaluable to me throughout the process.

After years of hearing their names at the family dinner table, it's been a pleasure to finally work firsthand with the terrific team at HarperCollins. I'd especially like to thank my editor, Toni Sciarra, for her excellent advice and keen eye for organization, and Mary Ellen O'Neill, my publisher, whose enthusiasm for this project was infectious from our first conversations. Thanks also to Smallwood and Stewart and Alexis Siroc for the masterful design work, and to Chesley McLaren, whose beautiful illustrations bring these pages alive.

None of this would have come into being without the brilliant foresight and tremendous hard work of my agent, Katherine Cowles. Thanks, Kitty!

Thanks also go to my aunt, Peggy Post, who has been so welcoming as I enter into her world of wedding etiquette. My parents, Tricia and Peter Post, and my sister, Lizzie Post, deserve thanks for their love, encouragement, and constant support and belief in my abilities—without which I don't know how I would have managed!

And of course a huge thank-you goes to the staff at the Emily Post Institute: Cindy Post Senning, Elizabeth Howell, Matt Bushlow, and especially Katherine Meyers, for being my unerring sounding board.

Thanks also to wedding consultant Mark Kingsdorf for his expert advice. And last but by no means least, a big thank you to all of my friends who shared their experiences and opinions with me. I'm so glad to be part of your lives; thank you for being part of mine.

FOREWORD
by Peggy Post

I'm delighted that my niece, Anna Post, has joined The Emily Post Institute full time as an etiquette expert and author. Anna has been involved with the Institute for years, starting as a summer intern. Her contributions have included researching the 17th edition of our flagship book, *Etiquette*, and answering hundreds of the letters that come to us via our Web site, www.emilypost.com. Anna and I have worked together numerous times, most recently at a major wedding show, and it's been a pleasure for me to experience firsthand the calm and factual manner in which she has helped brides and grooms solve their wedding etiquette dilemmas.

I'm now extremely pleased to tell you about her latest effort, *Emily Post's Wedding Parties*. What a fantastic job Anna has done on this, her first book! Besides drawing on her own experiences at the many weddings she's attended and participated in, she's also done a great deal of research into the variety of parties that surround today's weddings. *Emily Post's Wedding Parties* combines Anna's knowledge of "what's out there" with her knack of clearly explaining how the principles of etiquette—consideration, honesty, and respect—can be used to solve even the stickiest of quandaries that can arise when trying to ensure that everybody has a great time at a celebration. Anna has a wonderful way of offering practical solutions and applying her own fresh insights— all delivered with wit and wisdom in a uniquely personal voice—to today's etiquette situations.

At the Emily Post Institute, we're constantly fielding questions about weddings and the parties surrounding them. Who hosts? Who's invited? Is it ever okay to invite someone to a pre-wedding party if they're not invited to the wedding itself? What's the best way to word the invitation for a delayed wedding reception? Are gifts for the couple always necessary? How about gifts for the party's hosts? If you can't attend a shower, do you still have to send a gift?

These issues have been heightened by the increasing variety of wedding-related parties, and by the enormous role that travel now plays in these celebrations. Today, friends and relatives often live far away from the bride and groom. With people expending so much time and effort to get together, wedding-related events have become even more meaningful and special—which means there's even more incentive to make sure these parties are "just right." Whether you're hosting or attending an engagement party, looking for some new, fun tips for showers or bachelor/bachelorette parties, or preparing the wedding reception itself, Anna beautifully presents the reader with new party-planning ideas, while at the same time weaving in inspiration and etiquette advice for hosts, party guests, and the couple being honored.

Among other things, you'll learn:

* ✳ The timing of all the various wedding parties.

* ✳ Who to invite, and how and when to extend the invitations.

* ✳ What to do when the groom's parents want to throw a party to introduce the new bride-to-be to their friends in the months following the official engagement party.

* ✳ The etiquette of hosting attendants' parties in the week prior to the wedding.

* ✳ How pre- and post-wedding gatherings are taking on more significance for many couples and their guests—plus exciting ideas for extending the "wedding weekend," with events such as an impromptu pre-wedding barbecue, an after-the-reception party, or a farewell brunch.

* ✳ The do's and don'ts of belated receptions (now more popular than ever, thanks to the growing trend of destination weddings, which are often smaller than the typical wedding).

Whatever the occasion, *Emily Post's Wedding Parties* offers options, advice, and new ideas for the reader. I'm confident you'll agree that this book is truly a complete guide to all of the possible parties that may occur before, during, or after a wedding. These days, there really are more and more parties and celebrations surrounding weddings, and each one brings its own set of questions and dilemmas. Luckily, Anna Post has addressed these quandaries for you. You're holding the solutions in your hand!

INTRODUCTION

A wedding is an incredibly special time in two people's lives, and the various parties and celebrations that take place from engagement to "I do" are all important parts of this experience. These celebrations don't happen every day, however, so people understandably are often a bit fuzzy on the details. Should you bring a gift to an engagement party? Who's allowed to host a shower? How do you word an invitation to a wedding reception? Knowing the answers to these and other questions will help ensure that any wedding party you're hosting or attending goes smoothly for everyone involved—and that everyone's focus can be exactly where it should be: on celebrating the upcoming marriage of the bride and groom.

Emily Post's Wedding Parties covers all the wedding parties that may occur before and after a wedding ceremony. You'll learn about traditional wedding parties and the etiquette that comes with them. In addition, you'll get up-to-date info on all the latest trends in wedding-party customs and entertaining styles. If you're the one organizing a wedding party, you'll also find all the tips you need to plan the perfect event, from developing a timeline to handling invitations and RSVPs, signing contracts, hiring caterers, and even creating your own flower arrangements!

Each of the parties covered in this book is held for a good reason: Engagement parties celebrate a couple's declaration to marry; showers help the couple establish their new home together; bachelor and bachelorette parties mark the end of their single lives; farewell brunches are a lovely chance to say one last good-bye after the wedding reception; and I don't need to tell you what receptions are for! In their own way, each of these parties honors the couple's love and commitment to one another and helps prepare them for one of the biggest steps two people can take—their wedding and marriage—while also transforming two individuals and two families into one couple and one family, with everyone hopefully having loads of fun in the process!

On these sorts of occasions, people would often turn to my great-great-grandmother Emily Post for advice on how to do the *right* thing, the *traditional* thing. Her answers often surprised them, however—because Emily never believed in tradition for its own sake. In her view, good etiquette is not about doing what's "always been done"; it's about basing all of your words and actions on three key principles: consideration, honesty, and respect.

While these principles apply across life, they're especially useful for dealing with the many situations that occur between announcing the engagement and tossing the bouquet—and beyond. "Whenever two people come together and their behavior affects one another," said Emily Post, "you have etiquette. Etiquette is not some rigid code of manners; it's simply how persons' lives touch one another." She couldn't be more right—and a wedding is the ultimate definition of this: two people dedicating their lives to each other.

For this reason, it's no surprise that the majority of the questions we get here at the Emily Post Institute are about weddings. People want a unique, personalized wedding celebration, but they're also searching to find their place amid the different wedding traditions. Customs and cultures are constantly evolving, and these days an infinite number of special circumstances call for variations on "tradition" when planning wedding parties—including divorce, various combinations of different cultures and religions, and budgets and timetables of all sizes and lengths, to name a few. But by using the commonsense etiquette guidelines in this book as a blueprint, adding in your own unique variations, and always applying the principles of consideration, honesty, and respect, you'll find you can easily handle the most challenging situations with grace and humor.

Beyond the details of what to expect at all the different parties that occur in the process of getting married, I hope the entertaining tips in *Emily Post's Wedding Parties* give you the inspiration to throw a fabulous and memorable event. Remember, though, that while parties, presents, and pretty clothes may come to mind first, they're only symbols of what these gatherings are really all about: the ideals of commitment, mutual respect, and enduring love. And although this book addresses the parties surrounding a "traditional" marriage between a man and a woman, the etiquette advice and party ideas offered here apply equally to same-sex couples celebrating commitment ceremonies or civil unions. After all, the goal is the same: to throw parties for those near and dear to you, in order to share in a couple's happiness and commitment to one another. And what better reason to celebrate than that?

chapter one

we have an announcement to make

engagement parties

I've yet to meet a newly engaged couple who doesn't want to shout it to the world—and what better way than with a party? An **engagement party** is the first chance that a couple has to celebrate their decision to marry and to share their happiness with their family and friends. Engagement parties are not required, but they are traditional and very popular.

A GOOD PLACE TO START

Of course, the main point of an engagement party is to celebrate and announce the couple's engagement, but it's also a great chance for their families to get to know each other better. The same goes for friends: The couple's close friends may already know them as a twosome, but older friends may not. This party is also the moment when the engagement is officially "announced" (typically by the bride's father), and guests toast the couple's future.

An engagement party also builds anticipation and sets the tone for the wedding to come—something that should be kept in mind when planning the event. It doesn't have to "match" the wedding, but it should never outshine it: If the couple is planning an informal wedding, the engagement party should be on the casual side as well.

party timeline

The engagement party usually occurs fairly close to when the proposal is made and accepted—typically within a couple of months. At the very least, try to schedule it closer to the engagement than to the wedding. (If the engagement is extremely short, just do the best you can.) The one thing you *don't* want is for the engagement party to compete with the wedding. Short of that, there is no set time; just think about the length of the engagement and your calendar. My friend Ben got engaged in the fall, around the same time as his sister. They were both planning summer weddings, and it turned out that January was a great time for their parents to throw them a joint engagement party.

Remember to let close family and friends hear the good news from you first, in person or over the phone—*before* they get an invite in the mail for an engagement party. And it's okay to let everyone know even if the engagement party has to wait: "Hi, Uncle Dave—Jason and I got engaged! We're *so* happy! We wanted you to know now, even though we can't throw a party to celebrate until after he graduates from law school this spring."

Invitations should go out at least a few weeks in advance, to give invited guests a chance to arrange their schedules. If guests are coming from out of town, they'll need even more lead time—preferably four to six weeks.

A PERFECT ENGAGEMENT PARTY

I loved attending my friend Nell's engagement party. She held it at her mother's house and invited both family friends and her own friends from childhood, college, and post-college life. Having known her through all of these stages, it was fun for me to catch up with all the people I'd met through her over the years. It gave me a taste of how this kind of party can bring together many different parts of two people's lives—people who are all important to the couple but who wouldn't otherwise meet.

The party was a backyard affair on a summer evening. It was a little dressy, but not stuffy, with lots of flowers arranged from the bride's mother's garden, and heavy hors d'oeuvres from a local caterer, who stayed to help out at the event. There was a delicious cake with fresh berries for dessert, and plenty of champagne. About forty guests mingled in dresses and sport coats, talking and laughing with the blissful couple. Everyone had a fantastic time. The party was lovely, but not over the top, and suited the couple perfectly. Just as important, it was clear that the focus was on my friend and her fiancé sharing their news—and the resulting congratulations—with friends and family in a memorable way.

who hosts?

Traditionally, engagement parties are hosted by family members or close friends—most often the parents of the bride. If that's not an option, not to worry: Variations on this theme are increasingly common. In fact, it's perfectly fine for virtually anyone to host the celebration, with some couples even throwing engagement parties for themselves (see "Throw an Engagement Party for Yourself? Absolutely!" page 5).

There can also be more than one engagement party: For example, the bride's parents in Georgia might host one, inviting local friends and family, and the groom's parents in Oregon might do the same.

Hosts should *always* check with the couple in advance to find out what dates work best for them and to go over the guest list (see "Who's Invited?" below). Remember, too, that the bride's parents customarily have first shot at playing host: If the groom's parents want to throw an engagement party, they should check with the bride's parents to see if they're planning to hold one, too. If so, the bride's parents get first choice of date. The groom's parents should then schedule their party to *follow* it.

If some other relative or close friend is planning to throw an engagement party for the couple, they should check first with *both* sets of parents as well as the couple, to avoid stepping on anyone's toes.

who's invited?

Engagement parties are typically on the intimate side, with invitations going only to close friends and family. The definition of *close* is up to you—it could be 10 or 100. Parties with more extended friends and family are fine, too, but just remember that no matter the size of the guest list, **everyone invited to the engagement party must be invited to the wedding**. (For more on *why* this is, see Chapter 8, "Reading the Fine Print: Invitations," page 93.)

Throw an Engagement Party for Yourself?
Absolutely!

With so many people moving away from their hometowns and waiting until they're older to get engaged, many couples have well-established lives far from where they grew up. Throwing an engagement party yourself ensures that all your nearby friends get a chance to celebrate with you. (And of course, you're still free to attend any engagement parties hosted by other people in your honor!)

I recently had a fabulous time at a party hosted by two newly engaged friends in Washington, D.C., where we all worked and knew each other. The bride was originally from California, and the groom's family all lived in Pakistan. I'd known them only a year or so, and while I was happy to be at their engagement party, it's doubtful that I would have been invited—much less been able to attend—an engagement party thrown for them in California or Pakistan. This way, they got to celebrate their engagement with the friends they saw regularly, and everyone had a terrific time.

ask anna: does a super-short engagement still get a party?

Q: *My boyfriend and I just got engaged and are planning to get married in a month. Can we still have an engagement party?*

anna: Sure—just strive for balance: If you've only got a month between the engagement and the wedding, throw together an impromptu party as soon as possible—even within a week of deciding is okay. Just be aware that not every guest you invite will be able to attend on such short notice (that goes for the wedding, too).

WHAT KIND OF ENGAGEMENT PARTY SHOULD YOU HAVE?

There's no rule regarding what kind of engagement party to have. I've been to all types: big, small, formal, casual, parties for just the friends, and others with the entire extended families of the bride and groom. The best party will be one where everybody feels at ease and free to enjoy themselves, and where the couple and their hosts can focus on their guests rather than on making the party run smoothly. In deciding what type of party to have, think about the guest list, the venue, and any special touches that you'd like to incorporate. That should help you figure out whether you want to throw a cocktail party, a dinner party, or a skating party. Skating party, you ask? Read on....

the classic engagement party: an elegant affair

Things become classic for good reasons. While there's no rule as to what exactly makes a classic engagement party, this sort of event is typically held at the bride's parents' house or other private home (though a rented venue is fine, too) and features cocktails and hors d'oeuvres or a light buffet meal, with a dessert and coffee table set out later for guest to help themselves.

This style of party allows for a range of budgets—from homemade food and flower arrangements and CDs on the stereo to a caterer, professional florist, and entertainment by a small band. At the same time, it guarantees a relaxed setting where guests can mingle and chat with the happy couple.

think...

Cocktails, a buffet spread, hors d'oeuvres, dessert tables, and lots of champagne... party dresses and suits...mingling guests...subtle music in the background... and an announcement from the bride's father.

making it happen

- ✳ Invitations can be phoned but are probably printed or handwritten and should go out two to four weeks in advance.

- ✳ There's no rule against a seated dinner, but a buffet and/or hors d'oeuvres will help keep guests mingling and make it easier for the couple to chat with everyone.

- ✳ It's okay to handle the food on your own, but hiring a caterer is recommended.

- ✳ Dessert isn't mandatory, but it makes a sweet end to the evening.

- ✳ Flowers are optional, but they help set the tone for the party.

- ✳ Music is also optional, but it's a great idea; the hosts can either turn up the stereo or go all out with live musicians.

- ✳ If you want to ensure dancing, mention it on the invite and plan your music accordingly.

- ✳ Attention, fathers of the bride! Be prepared to say a few words announcing your daughter's engagement (see Chapter 11, "Cheers! Making Toasts," page 139).

- ✳ Arrange for parking and a coat rack, if needed.

the intimate dinner party: keeping it personal

A dinner party with close friends and family, held at a restaurant or in someone's home (where the meal can be catered or home-cooked), is an intimate way to celebrate an engagement and often costs less as well. This style of party is ideal for any group small enough to be comfortably seated at one table.

think...

Candlelight and a cozy atmosphere with your closest friends and family...stories from your childhood...warmhearted toasts...and lingering over coffee.

making it happen

- Invitations can be printed but are probably handwritten or phoned and should be extended two to four weeks in advance.

- The meal can be home-cooked, catered, or held at a restaurant.

- Consider a beautiful floral arrangement in the center of the table and a few blooms for the powder room.

- Don't forget candles!

- If the party is held in someone's home, plan CDs or an i-Pod playlist in advance, so you can simply press "play" when the party starts.

One emerging trend is to link the engagement party to a place or theme that's significant to the couple. The results can be *awww*-inspiring. Did the couple go ice-skating on their first date? Hold a skating party at a local rink, with warm drinks and dessert. Do they both love wine? Find an *enoteca* or wine bar to host the party at, or create your own sampling at home with bottles of wine from special occasions they've shared. Did he propose on a trip to Hawaii? Host a luau!

You get the idea. It doesn't have to be extreme, either: One couple had an unforgettable engagement party spooning up sundaes with their guests at the ice cream parlor where they first fell in love.

ask anna: long-distance invitation

Q: *When planning an engagement party, should I invite guests who live far away and would have to fly in for the party?*

anna: Typically, no. The exception to this rule is a best friend or favorite relative who lives far away but who you know would feel hurt if they *weren't* invited. In this case, an invitation is called for—even if you know they aren't likely to attend.

DO GUESTS HAVE TO BRING A GIFT TO THE ENGAGEMENT PARTY?

The short answer is *no*. The classic rule of thumb is that gifts are *not* given to celebrate an engagement unless you're an especially close friend or family member. Even then, the gift should be given discreetly and should never be opened at the party, to avoid embarrassing other guests who (quite appropriately) didn't bring anything.

These days, however, the trend is changing. While "no gifts" is still the rule in many areas, in some places—particularly in big cities and in the northeastern United States—giving engagement gifts is becoming more and more common. For now, the best advice is to check with your host to find out what's expected.

If you *do* give an engagement gift, remember that it's intended as a gesture of affection and needn't be expensive or elaborate: A nice bottle of wine will do just fine. If you're stumped, think about what the couple enjoys doing together—or pick something that has special meaning for you. I love giving vases made by Simon Pearce, a glass-blowing company in my home state of Vermont.

MAKING IT OFFICIAL

Even if everyone knows the big news, it's customary (though optional) for the father of the bride—or some other suitable person in his absence—to "officially" announce the engagement at the engagement party (see "Three Parties Where Toasts Are a Must," page 139).

CHOOSING AN ENGAGEMENT GIFT

from you:	what it says:
Vases, pretty bowls	sweet and classic
Gift certificate to a restaurant	versatile and sure to please
Picture of the couple in an engraved frame	personal touch
Two champagne flutes and a bottle of champagne	sophisticated
Beautiful throw blanket	cozy and thoughtful
Picnic basket with picnic set for two inside	comfy and down to earth
Cookbook	for the motivated couple
Massage oils	ooh la la—a little racy
Gift certificate to a spa	indulgent—and why not?
Weekend at a bed and breakfast	extravagant!
Antique cake knife	you love weddings
Cute kitchen accessories	girly
Set of Pilsner glasses	you're a guy
Set of monogrammed Pilsner glasses	you're a guy with a girlfriend
Flowers	you're sorry you couldn't be there

the written word versus word of mouth

When spreading news of your engagement to friends and acquaintances, word of mouth is the classic method. Above all, it's considered inappropriate to send out printed announcements. The reason: A mailed announcement might be mistaken to mean that a wedding invitation will follow. That's why many couples choose to publish an announcement of their engagement in their local newspaper. One cautionary note: If you're planning a surprise announcement, make sure any newspaper announcements are slated to appear *after* the party!

surprise—we're getting married!

Some couples choose to make a surprise announcement of their engagement. In this case, the party invitations are simply for dinner, cocktails, brunch, or whatever type of party is being planned. Then, once all the guests have arrived, the bride's father or fiancé (or someone else close to her) makes a little speech and drops the big news. If you go this road, just be sure that everyone present will be on board with the idea once they know. Otherwise, the party could go south fast—hardly the way you want to start off your engagement!

"congratulations!"...or not?

It used to be considered impolite to say "Congratulations!" to a newly engaged woman, since it was thought that this word carried the snarky implication that she'd finally managed to snag herself a man. Preferred expressions included "Best wishes" and "I'm so pleased to hear your wonderful news." Luckily, times change. You'll be glad to know that today it's perfectly okay to wish a bride-to-be well with that once-taboo word. After all, it's the underlying sentiment—that her friends and family are happy for her and her fiancé—that's most important. So...congratulations!

shower oohs and ahhs and (bachelor)ette party last hurrahs

The weeks and months following the engagement party are usually taken up with a dizzying amount of details involved in planning the wedding itself. Fortunately, just when it all might start to seem overwhelming, tradition throws you a couple of lifelines— parties that allow you to step off the roller coaster, let down your hair (or put your feet up), and concentrate on relaxing and enjoying yourself with your closest friends.

I'm referring, of course, to **wedding showers** and **(bachelor)ette parties**. Although the original idea behind these parties was to engage in some serious bonding with your girlfriends, this time-honored approach is in the throes of a makeover. While many brides are still embracing the all-female tradition, others are opening these once girl-only gatherings to (gasp!) guys as well. And why not? Most of us have as many guy friends as we do girls, and these parties are all about having a great time with your friends—whether they're girls or guys.

SHOWERS IN THE FORECAST

The bridal shower is the ultimate "girl" moment of the pre-wedding process, summoning up images of tea parties, finger sandwiches, and lots of ribbons and bows—but showers can be so much more than that these days. You're not the girly-girl type? Opt for a chic wine and cheese party, where everyone brings a bottle of their favorite vintage. Can't stand to leave your man? Coed "Jack and Jill" showers are all the rage. Showers can also be a ton of fun to plan, with so many possibilities for creating something just right for the bride's lifestyle—and the groom's!

party timeline

Ideally, showers are held anywhere from two months to two weeks before the wedding. Any closer to the big day and it just gets too hectic for everyone. Any further out, and the shower won't build momentum toward the wedding.

who hosts?

In years past, close family members of the bride (her mother, sisters, aunts, and so on) wouldn't have *dreamed* of throwing her a shower. Why? Because the main point of a shower is to give gifts to the bride, and it seemed inappropriate for the bride or her close family to host such a party—as though they might be *asking* for gifts.

These days, while it's still considered a faux pas for an engaged couple to throw their own shower—the asking-for-gifts thing again—pretty much anyone else can host one. In fact, as long as they aren't inviting everyone under the sun or throwing multiple showers, it's often easiest for the bride's mother or sister or aunt to play host. Sometimes several of the bride's friends or relatives may host the shower together—sharing the expenses and the organizing.

Legend has it that long ago in Holland, a young Dutch girl fell in love with a poor miller. Her rich father opposed the match and threatened to withhold her dowry if his daughter went through with the wedding. The couple married anyway, but her lack of dowry left them practically penniless. The other townspeople took pity on the miller, who had always been kind to them, and his young bride, and they came to the mill carrying gifts for the couple's household. The girl's father was so ashamed when he saw this outpouring of kindness and generosity that his heart melted: He bought a house for them and threw a feast so that everyone could celebrate their marriage. Needless to say, everyone lived happily ever after.

From this beautiful tale comes the wedding shower as we know it today—a chance for close friends and family to shower the couple with good wishes and useful presents, as they begin to establish their household together. Of course, the emphasis should be on wishing the couple well, rather than on the presents. That said, however, the rule is: Unless guests are specifically asked not to bring gifts, it's understood that if you attend a wedding shower, you should always come with a gift.

who's invited?

Showers are usually intimate affairs. While the exact size of the event is up to the host, the idea is not to invite the entire guest list for the wedding. (This really *would* look like a grab for gifts.) Usually the guest list is made up of close female friends and relatives of the bride. The one rule of thumb: **However big or small the guest list ends up being, anyone invited to the shower should also be invited to the wedding.** The only exception to this is when coworkers throw an office shower (see "All-Staff Memo: Office Shower Etiquette" on page 23).

ask anna: bridesmaids, relax!

Q: *I've heard that in addition to our other duties, the bridesmaids are supposed to host a shower for the bride. Is that true?*

anna: No. Contrary to popular belief, the maid/matron of honor and the bridesmaids are *not* required to host a shower as part of their official responsibilities (though they can if they want to). So all you frantic bridesmaids out there can heave a sigh of relief—you're off the hook on this one! ❀

SHOWER THEMES:
From Lingerie to the Great Outdoors

One common approach is a theme shower, which determines the kinds of gifts guests give and offers a fun way to personalize the shower. A few suggestions follow; of course, you can go with any theme that fits the bride and the shower's hosts—or no theme at all, other than having good time.

theme	gift ideas
Wine and…(cheese/beer/music/cigars, etc.): *This shower can round out the couple's collection of wines and whichever add-on they like best.*	Guests should bring a bottle of wine and/or whatever else is requested—fine cheeses, a case of microbrew beer, a favorite CD, or a box of cigars.
Tea party: *This shower is great for helping the couple stock up on goodies for their morning coffee, afternoon tea, or evening mug of cocoa.*	Presents might be nice teas, coffees, cocoas, mugs, coffeemakers or coffee grinders, packages of fancy cookies, serving trays, teapots, or teacups.
Around the world: *For world gourmets or travel enthusiasts. This party lends itself well to a cocktail party with hors d'oeuvres from all around the world.*	Gifts might be gourmet international foods or wines, travel accessories, CDs of world music, or beautiful books on travel and other cultures.
The great outdoors: *This shower supplies the adventurous couple with presents to help keep them moving in the wilderness. The invitation should indicate what activities they like to do but, as always, should not suggest gifts.*	Depending on what the couple enjoys doing, guests might bring them camping equipment, fleece blankets, matching ski hats, or golf clothes, to name a few.
How does your garden grow? *For the gardening couple, this party will nurture their green thumbs. The garden shower theme makes for a nice garden party or tea party.*	Guests can bring gifts like tin watering cans, garden tools, packets of flower and/or vegetable seeds, bird feeders, or sets of his-and-hers garden gloves.
Tools and gadgets: *Especially great for coed parties, this shower supplies the couple with fun tools and gadgets for the house.*	Think Brookstone meets Home Depot. Gifts might be a travel alarm clock, a mini blow torch for crème brûlées, or an all-in-one tool kit.
Entertainment: *The idea here is to provide the couple with entertaining things to do.*	Gifts might be DVDs, CDs, movie tickets, museum passes, restaurant gift certificates, puzzles or games, books, journals, or magazine subscriptions.
Room of the house: *Guests are asked to bring a gift for a specific room of the house.*	Most rooms are fairly self-explanatory, though I did once get stumped by the home office; a nice desk set, a cool paperweight, an assortment of beautiful note cards, or pair of picture frames could all see you through.

theme	gift ideas
Hours of the day: *Guests are given an hour of the day for which to buy the couple a present.*	8 AM guests might give a set of egg cups or a juicer, while 8 PM guests might give a CD of dinner music or a set of beautiful candles for the dinner table.
Months of the year: *Guests are assigned a month of the year and buy the couple a present appropriate to that month.*	Guests with January might give cocoas or matching cashmere socks; a guest with July might give a picnic basket or croquet set.
Letters of the alphabet: *Guests are allotted a letter of the alphabet and buy the couple a present that starts with that letter.*	Guests given the letter s might bring presents such as a collection of gourmet salsas or a gardening spade and seeds.
Bed and breakfast: *Guests are asked to bring gifts for the kitchen or bedroom. This is a great shower to throw as a brunch!*	Gifts should be for use in the bedroom or kitchen but can go beyond the obvious items if you're feeling creative, such as a set of books for bedside reading or a poker set for playing a game around the kitchen table. Just be sure your explanation makes sense, so it's clear you're still playing along.
Lingerie party: *Not for the faint of heart! The idea here is to keep the spark alive in the bedroom. A word of warning: Choose your audience carefully with this one.*	All kinds of lingerie, from negligees and bra and panty sets to chemises and camisoles, slips, garters, and fancy stockings. If you're not comfortable buying the lacy stuff, cozy pajamas, robes, or slippers are always a welcome alternative.
Spa shower: *A shower to indulge and pamper the senses.*	Gifts should pamper the bride and groom, such as bubble bath, scented candles, massage oils, or robes.

SHOWER THEMES ON A BUDGET

Between throwing down for wedding gifts and chipping in on expenses for showers and other parties, people near and dear to the bride and groom can end up spending quite a bit in the name of the couple's lifelong happiness. That's why I love showers that focus on gifts that don't require a huge bank account. In fact, these types of showers often inspire greater thought—and more interesting results—than simply picking something out of a registry. Here are some terrific ideas for low-cost shower themes.

theme	gift ideas
Stock the bar: *Best served as a cocktail party.*	Gifts might be bottles of wines, liquors or liqueurs, wine or cocktail glasses, tumblers, mixers, swizzle sticks, coasters, bar equipment, bar towels, or cocktail napkins.
Recipes: *Send note cards or matching paper with the invitations, asking everyone to write down their favorite recipe for the couple. These can then be put into a recipe box or photo album for the couple to use.*	A favorite recipe. A nice to touch is to have everyone explain on the card why it's their favorite (their grandmother's apple pie; the easiest dinner ever; the pancake batter recipe they made up themselves).
Labor of love: *Guests are asked to pledge a service to the couple.*	Promises might be for an afternoon of gardening, baking them cookies, or washing their car.
Handmade: *This shower has a very personal touch, while also helping to keep gift budgets low.*	Gifts can be anything, so long as they are handmade—by you, not a master wood carver.
Sage advice: *Guests are asked to write out a piece of marriage advice. My advice: As with the recipes, send out standard-sized note cards or paper that can be collected to make a book or mounted in a photo album.*	Words of wisdom might range from sage to sassy, including maxims like "Never go to bed angry" or "Remember: she's always right."
Memories: *Write a favorite memory you have of the bride. At the end, the bride will have a beautiful collection of favorite memories from her friends and family.*	Examples might include the first time you met her, the moment you knew you'd be friends for life, or the day she told you she got engaged.

"JACK AND JILL" SHOWERS

Coed showers, often called "Jack and Jill" showers, are basically the same as a traditional shower, except that they include the groom and his guy friends, too. Most of the themes described above can be easily modified for both the bride *and* groom. One coed theme that I *don't* recommend is the lingerie party. The concept might seem amusing and even provocative at first glance, but the fact is that this sort of party is very bride-oriented, and if the groom's friends are there, too, it could get uncomfortable fast for everyone involved.

Jack and Jill showers really get fun when it comes time for the games. These usually involve asking the couple questions that center on "how well do you *really* know your spouse-to-be?" This requires a little preparation, of course, since someone will have to ask both the bride and the groom a number of questions in advance and keep track of the answers ("What's his favorite movie?" "When is her birthday?" "Where did you share your first kiss?" and so on). Keep the questions light, and focus on subjects that can withstand a little teasing, in case someone *does* happen to come up with the wrong answer.

SHOWER GIFTS

Should you bring a gift to a shower? Yes—unless the invitation clearly states "no gifts." (Those who can't attend the shower don't have to send a gift—though many people will choose to send one anyway.) If there's a registry or a theme, try to keep to it; it's more fun if everyone plays along. Shower presents don't need to be expensive or elaborate. Think along the lines of things for their new home, either useful or frivolous. A few ideas are listed below. (For more gift ideas, see "Shower Themes: From Lingerie to the Great Outdoors," page 16.)

All shower gifts should be opened at the party and passed around. Keep pacing in mind, so that everyone has a chance to have their gift opened, appreciated, and fully oohed and ahhed over.

"just what we needed"	fun and frivolous
Coffeemaker	antique coffee spoons
Set of colorful dishtowels and pot holders	funny doormat
Salad bowl	set of exotic spices
Hand towels for a powder room	pretty soaps
Tumblers for the bar	goofy swizzle sticks and cocktail napkins
Set of gardening tools	potted orchid
Cookbook	pancake mix and Vermont maple syrup

ask anna: can I list registry info on the shower invitation?

Q: *I'm hosting a shower for a friend, who has set up a registry for this. Can I let guests know about the registry on the invitation?*

anna: No, not on the actual invitation. Doing so is considered tacky, as though presents are the *only* purpose of the party. Unlike wedding invitations, however, it is okay to include a separate sheet of paper along with the invitation, letting guests know where the bride is registered. This may seem like splitting hairs, but the end result is that the focus is kept on celebrating the upcoming wedding with the bride or couple, rather than on the gifts.

thanks—and thanks again

Finally, **all gifts should be acknowledged with a handwritten thank-you note from the engaged couple, even if the giver has already been thanked in person.** Most people expect a thank-you note when they give a gift. Sending one ensures that no one is left confused or offended. Just think of it as good practice for all those wedding-present thank-yous, as well as a chance to buy some chic note cards!

all-staff memo: office shower etiquette

Since most of us spend so much time with our colleagues at work, an office shower is a great way to celebrate your upcoming wedding with your workmates, without necessarily inviting them to the wedding itself. (Office showers are the *only* occasion when the rule of "anyone invited to the shower should also be invited to the wedding" doesn't apply.)

An office shower is never something that the bride or couple requests; it happens when the bride's (or groom's) colleagues offer to throw one for the couple. Since most offices are coed, it's nice to include both the bride- and groom-to-be in the event. This is probably not the time for themes—the party is taking place at an office, after all, usually as a break from the workday, so it's best to keep it simple.

If the office is small, be sure that everyone is invited. If it's large, use good judgment, perhaps limiting the invited guests to the bride's department, floor, or team. Printed invitations aren't necessary; an e-mail, phone call, or personally delivered message with the details is fine.

At most office showers, colleagues all chip in together for a gift. The collecting of funds needs to be handled carefully: It's best to let people know there's a collection envelope at a designated person's desk, rather than going around from person to person, which really puts people on the spot. While a suggested amount is fine, keep it low, and never make it mandatory that people contribute in order to be able to attend the shower. Nor should anyone ever be given a hard time for donating less than others or nothing at all. In fact, a truly thoughtful "designated collector" will avoid ever mentioning who gave how much.

about that surprise shower you're planning . . .

Remember that *Friends* episode where Courteney Cox's character badmouths all her acquaintances, only to have them all come crawling out of the woodwork around her—literally—having heard every awful word while they were waiting to surprise her with a shower? It's a classic—classically mortifying, that is!

While it's doubtful that any real surprise shower would ever backfire quite that badly, surprises are always a risky business. Suppose the bride has something come up at the last minute or isn't dressed appropriately? Or what if people are invited whom she wasn't planning on inviting to the wedding? Even worse, what if she didn't really want a shower at all? Unless you're absolutely sure that springing a surprise shower will be an unquestionable hit, opt for some sort of smaller surprise instead—such as

- A special guest from out of town (just be sure she or he is someone she's inviting to the wedding!) or even her fiancé
- Photos from the bride's (or groom's) past
- An arrangement of her favorite flowers that she can take home with her

the etiquette of multiple showers

Multiple showers are okay, but be sure to invite different guests to each party. Only close family, friends, and the wedding party may be invited to more than one shower.

As a guest, if you *are* invited to more than one shower, you only need to bring a gift to the first one—that goes for members of the wedding party, too. (If you don't want to come to the second empty-handed, you can always bring something inexpensive such as a small bouquet, chocolates, or even some homemade goodies.) Brides: If you have a guest in this position, it's nice to make a mention of their previous gift at the second shower, so it's clear to other guests that the person already gave something.

(BACHELOR)ETTE PARTIES:
One Last Hurrah

I have one word for you: *strippers*. Oh, come on, it's what you were thinking, too—admit it! While some people do choose to go down that road, there are tons of other ways today that both girls and guys are choosing to let their hair down—and believe it or not, everyone's clothes are staying on.

From Cosmos to Camping Trips. The bachelorette party is the bride's last hurrah, a swan song to her single life—and as such, the ultimate girls' night out is often the order of the day. Think dinner at a nice restaurant and an evening of drinks with lots of cosmos (à la *Sex and the City*). Depending on what the bride likes to do, the party could also be combined with a trip to a concert or sports event or a group activity such as bowling or golf. Basically, you can do anything that allows you to spend some quality time with your best friends.

One great alternative to a night of debauchery is to gather everybody for a spa day, where you all enjoy a healthy lunch, get pampered, and *relax*. Or why not dress up and go to a fancy hotel for a high tea? Then there's always the "great escape": a weekend away at the beach, camping, or skiing.

Of course, the most decadent classic blowout (bachelor)ette weekend is, and probably always will be: Las Vegas. It's all up to your interests, budget, and schedules.

If the bride is a good sport, the party planners might consider a scavenger hunt in which clues are set out for the bride, leading her from place to place. These clues can be designed simply to move the night along, to lead the group to favorite places you went on girls' nights in the past, or to take the party to locations that hold special significance to the bride and her fiancé.

Another twist on this game is to write out tasks for the bride to perform. As the party progresses, she draws the tasks from a hat. The night I did this with friends, we gave the bride assignments such as "serenade a guy," "get the bartender to let you make a drink behind the bar," and "get a guy to carry you over the threshold of the bar." A complete trooper, she accomplished every single one!

party timeline

Bachelorette (and bachelor) parties are usually held anywhere from a week to two months before the wedding. This extra lead time is both in case a little recovery time is needed and also because life is sure to get super busy in the days immediately preceding the wedding.

Some brides double their fun by scheduling a shower and their bachelorette party over the same weekend, so that out-of-town friends can participate without having to pay for two trips. I once had a great weekend in New York City, taking a soon-to-be-married friend out for her bachelorette dinner and drinks on a Saturday night, and then attending her shower the next afternoon. Just watch out for hangovers, especially if your mother is going to be at the shower the next day!

who hosts?

Though the bachelorette party is often organized by the maid of honor and the bride's other attendants, this party can really be thrown by any of the bride's friends (in close consultation with the bride, of course). Bear in mind that this is *not* a "must-do" party but a purely optional indulgence. So if people's budgets or time are so tight that a bachelorette party feels like a strain, no one should be guilt-tripped into hosting one.

who's invited?

Typically, the guest list includes the maid of honor, the bridesmaids, and the bride's close female friends and relatives (usually those near to her in age—though mothers and aunts have been known to make an appearance, too). Since the night is all about celebrating with your closest friends, the number of guests shouldn't be too large—a dozen or so is often plenty.

Male friends of the bride can also be invited, if she wants—just consider the context first. A spa day? Probably not. Dinner out? Sure! (Guys are mixing it up these days, too; I once attended a bachelor party for a good male friend who invited both his guy and girl friends to a fabulous steak and lobster dinner.)

ask anna: at a bachelorette party, who pays?

Q: I'm planning a bachelorette party for my best friend. Since I'm technically the host, am I expected to pick up the tab for everyone?

anna: The bachelorette party is one event where the hosts aren't expected to foot the bill for everyone. Typically, everyone chips in to cover the cost of the bride's dinner and drinks, since she's the one being honored. Any arrangement you come up with is fine, however—just be sure that everyone is on the same page before the night begins.

Bachelorette Party Gifts. "No gifts" is generally the rule at a bachelorette party. One very popular custom, however, is to give the bride an inexpensive little something to commemorate the evening—usually a token like a T-shirt (or perhaps a more intimate garment) saying "Bride-to-Be" or "Taken." Take the time to pick out something that's both funny and still in good taste.

AND WHAT ARE THE GUYS UP TO?

Ever wondered what the boys might be getting up to without the girls around? Here are a few ideas if your fiancé is stumped on what to do for his own last hurrah:

✱ Smoking jacket optional: A steak dinner, followed by cigars and liqueurs.

✱ Poker night: Keep it casual with beer, pizza, and a poker game.

✱ Take me out to the ball game: Make a day of going to a sports event.

✱ Manly men in the great outdoors: Head off for a weekend of camping, boating, or golf, to name a few activities.

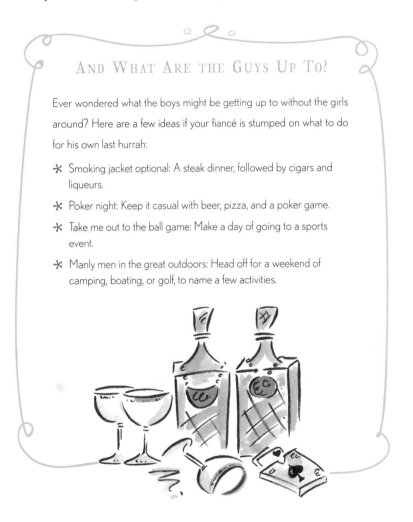

The Latest Trend. At the stroke of midnight, the party will turn…coed? Some couples combine the best of both worlds by starting out with separate (bachelor)ette parties for the bride and groom, then having everyone in both groups meet up later for drinks. This is a great way for the couple to enjoy some quality time with "just the girls" and "just the guys," and then end the night by celebrating with all of their friends together.

a note on comfort levels, good taste, and keeping everyone safe

All joking aside, bachelor and bachelorette parties are *not* the time for strippers and two-day hangovers; they are about celebrating and sharing in the excitement of the upcoming wedding. Whatever entertainment is planned, it shouldn't embarrass, humiliate, or endanger anyone. Emily Post herself was against Prohibition, but I can safely say she would have been all *for* designated drivers. (I know I am!) So be sure to have one (or plan to call taxis) if significant drinking is involved. After all, your single life has been stylish, fabulous, and tasteful—so why not end strong on the same note?

building the anticipation

wedding-week events and the rehearsal dinner

From the traditional **rehearsal dinner** to new takes on the **bridesmaids' party** and **groom's dinner,** the various wedding-week parties are all intended to help the couple and their nearest and dearest make the most of this interlude by spending some quality time together before all the other wedding guests descend.

WEDDING-WEEK EVENTS

More and more, the week before the wedding is becoming an opportunity for extra events, as close family, the wedding party, and perhaps even some guests start arriving early. All of these parties are optional, and at first glance they may seem to add unnecessary complication to this busy week. Keep in mind, though, that these gatherings are meant to be casual, relaxed get-togethers—nothing more. Besides, scheduling some downtime in between last-minute fittings and checking in with the florist is a great way to keep you and your attendants fresh and ready to smile for the camera on your wedding day.

Take a Moment to Smell Those Roses You've Ordered. A wedding is about two people committing themselves to each other, and I don't need to tell you that this is a huge step to take. But weddings are also a time to recognize the other important relationships in your life. Wedding-week parties offer a wonderful opportunity to spend some special time with the people who mean the most to you.

party timeline

These parties can occur anytime during the week or so before the wedding, except the night before—that's for the rehearsal dinner.

who hosts?

The bridesmaids' party is often hosted by the maid or matron of honor with the help of the bridesmaids, but it might also be hosted by the bride, usually with her mother. The groom's dinner is almost always hosted by the best man. Any other parties are most often arranged by the couple, although—given how busy they're sure to be—any combination of the attendants, parents, or even siblings helping out is okay. The idea is simply that these events are fun opportunities to begin celebrating.

who's invited?

Of course, the members of your wedding party are on the guest list for the attendants' parties. As for the other parties in this section, who gets invited is up to the engaged couple and may depend in large part on who's in town already and what kind of event you're thinking of throwing.

When inviting your attendants to these parties, bear in mind that people need enough advance warning to make the appropriate travel arrangements. It's probably best to talk over the idea of these gatherings with your attendants at the time the wedding invitations are sent out, then send the wedding-week party invitations as soon as your plans are confirmed.

are gifts given?

Gifts aren't given at the wedding-week parties—unless the bride and groom prefer to exchange any gifts they might be giving with their attendants at these parties rather than at the rehearsal dinner. Either time is fine; it's up to the couple. (For more on gifts exchanged between the couple and their attendants, see Chapter 9, "All About Party Gifts—and Those All-Important Thank-Yous," page 111.)

WEDDING-WEEK PARTIES

Following is a list of the most popular types of wedding-week parties. Some, like the bridesmaids' party, are traditional. Others, like a golf day, are modern additions. Whether or not you choose to throw any of them is up to you.

bridesmaids' party

The bridesmaids' party is usually held either a day or two before the wedding or on the morning of the wedding itself—in which case the party might become a trip to the salon or a visit from a makeup artist and/or hairdresser. The bridesmaids' party is traditionally hosted by the bride's attendants and is usually organized by the maid or matron of honor. In some communities, however, the bride and her mother host the party as a thank-you to the bridesmaids for their hard work and many contributions. I especially love this concept—since being a bridesmaid nowadays can consume quite a lot of time and money, this is a nice gesture of appreciation. (I added it up once and realized that when all was said and done, I'd spent a total of more than $1,000 being someone's bridesmaid. She's one of my very best friends, so I didn't begrudge this amount, but the fact remains that being in the wedding party can be very expensive.) A luncheon, brunch, or afternoon tea is traditional, but a dinner or cocktail party is equally nice, either at home or at a restaurant. As mentioned above, this can be a good opportunity for the bride to exchange any gifts with her attendants.

groom's dinner

The same concept goes for the guys. The idea is for the best man, groomsmen, and ushers to get together to honor the groom. And while in this case tradition calls for a dinner, any way they want to celebrate is fine, including a lunch or brunch, or even meeting for beers at a local pub. The gathering is usually organized by the best man and held in the days immediately preceding the wedding. The event can be as formal or casual as the hosts like. As with the bridesmaids' luncheon, it can also be a good time for exchanging any gifts between the groom and groomsmen.

twists on tradition

Both of these parties can be modified (or added to) to include anything from a game of croquet or golf to an afternoon of boating, hiking, or picnicking, to name a few. Go with what suits you best. Any activity that lets everyone take advantage of their time together and have a great time is fair game.

THE SKY'S THE LIMIT

There's really no limit to the kinds of parties that can be thrown in the days leading up a wedding. Here are a few ideas to get you started:

Croquet

Spa

Golf (or mini-golf)

Sailing

A community-service day

Beach day (just wear sun-screen—no one wants to have a sunburn in wedding photos!)

A hike

Flag football (no injuries, please!)

Ski day

A boat or helicopter tour (if you're in an exotic location)

A picnic

Bowling

---

what to do with out-of-town guests

The question of what to do with out-of-town guests is a good one—the concern being that they may end up sitting bored in their hotel rooms with nothing to do and nowhere to go prior to the wedding. In truth, however, your out-of-town guests almost certainly will be glad to have some free time to explore the area and rest from their trip. You do not have an obligation to entertain them, nor should they expect to be invited to the rehearsal dinner.

That's not to say that it isn't perfectly okay to include out-of-town guests at the rehearsal dinner, if you wish (and if budgets allow). But since rehearsal dinners are traditionally more intimate affairs, the preferred approach is to provide them with the names of some good local restaurants they might want to try that evening—along with a message stating that you're sorry you can't be with them that night but are looking forward to seeing them the following day. This way, out-of-town guests have plenty of options for enjoying their evening, while the bride and groom are free to focus on the rehearsal dinner.

the out-of-towners party

Another great alternative is to go the extra mile and arrange a separate party or dinner for out-of-towners. Held on the same evening as the rehearsal dinner, it gives guests a chance to catch up or get acquainted while the bride and groom and their attendants and close family are busy at the rehearsal dinner.

The party is often given by multiple hosts, so that they can share the expenses and work, and might be held at a private home or in a club or restaurant. Invitations should be sent out well in advance so that guests can plan their travel accordingly. If this event seems just too much to pull off, or if you don't have a host or hosts at hand who might fit the bill, then any arrangements you can make—such as setting up a buffet at the guests' hotel (which could range from drinks and snacks to a full dinner)—is sure to be appreciated and would be a gracious welcome.

When my friends Ken and Jessica got married, I drove nine hours to be there. Arriving at my hotel room, I was so grateful to discover a pretty paper bag filled with fruit, bottled water, mints, granola bars, and a lovely note from the couple. This sort of generous gesture is sure to make any out-of-town guest feel welcome— and the size or expense doesn't matter; it's the spirit of inclusiveness that counts.

THE REHEARSAL DINNER

I can't tell you how many times people have told me that the rehearsal dinner is their favorite part of a wedding—and I often couldn't agree more! It's a time to celebrate the upcoming wedding in a relaxed atmosphere, without the pomp and ceremony reserved for the wedding day. Everyone is arriving fresh and excited, and since rehearsal dinners are almost always limited to the couple's closest friends and family, the atmosphere is more personal and private than the wedding reception.

I should add here that rehearsal dinners are actually optional—so if for any reason the couple doesn't wish to have one, their choice should be respected. That being said, it's a rare wedding that doesn't feature some sort of dinner for close family and friends the night before the big event.

Practice Makes Perfect. The actual wedding rehearsal is fairly cut and dried, with everyone in the wedding party walking through the ceremony so they'll know what to do the next day. But what fun would it be if everyone just went home afterward? The rehearsal dinner is the perfect way to keep the rehearsal from ending anticlimactically. More important, however, the rehearsal dinner is the time when the families and attendants are formally welcomed, and it also offers everyone the perfect opportunity to gather together and begin the wedding celebration.

party timeline

It almost always makes the most sense to hold the rehearsal dinner the night before the wedding. Not only is this convenient for everyone but it also helps build momentum for the wedding ceremony and reception the next day—sort of like a sneak preview of what's to come. And what better feeling than to be at a terrific party, surrounded by people you love, knowing that you'll see them all again for the wedding and another great party tomorrow?

who hosts?

It's become customary, though not obligatory, for the groom's family to host the rehearsal dinner, and they should always be given first crack at taking charge of the event. This night is their chance to make a major contribution to the tone of the wedding. A couple of realities to consider: often, the groom's family isn't from the town or city where the wedding is being held; they'll also want to avoid stepping on the toes of the bride's family, who most likely have been immersed in planning the wedding itself.

Bringing the Families Together

The main focus of the rehearsal dinner is about bringing two families together as one. At my cousin Peter's wedding to his wife Elizabeth, her family met our family for the first time at the rehearsal dinner. While Elizabeth and Peter got their fair share of toasts, glasses were also raised for a number of lovely speeches about these two families coming together.

The best thing the couple can do to help make this happen is to be sure that everyone is introduced to each other. You'll be busy chatting with everyone anyway, so all you have to do is remember to be a little thoughtful as you mingle—giving a little nudge here and there with the introductions. (For tips on how to make introductions, see Chapter 10, "It Takes Two: The Perfect Host, the Perfect Guest," page 127.) Mixing up the families a little bit when arranging the table seating can help as well; just be considerate about who you pair up with whom. Seating the bride's twenty-year-old sister next to the groom's grandmother might be fine—and I'm sure they'd both be polite about it—but the bride's sister would probably have a lot more fun sitting with the groom's single male cousin who's attending med school. (For more on this, see "Priority Seating," page 131.)

Since the bride and groom are literally the common link between the families, they can be very helpful by arranging a time for everyone to talk about the rehearsal dinner plans, whether in person or over the phone. Specifically, the groom's family will need to know

- Recommendations for appropriate places in town to host the dinner (preferably close to the rehearsal site)
- The time and location of the rehearsal
- The style of the reception, including colors, size, and level of formality (it never hurts to complement the colors and style of the reception, though this is in no way required)
- The names and mailing addresses of wedding guests who will be invited to the rehearsal dinner

These conversations are also opportunities for the two families to get to know each other better. The groom's family can set the tone by being open to suggestions and advice; the bride's family can return the favor by offering to help with local details and by remembering that the groom's family is ultimately in the driver's seat on this one. The only rule to keep in mind when planning the dinner: Don't outshine the reception to come.

when someone else hosts

Typically, the groom's family chooses to host the rehearsal dinner, or at least to foot the lion's share of the bill. Still, it's perfectly okay to have a rehearsal dinner even if the groom's family can't or chooses not to host it. In this case, the couple should decide whether they want to host themselves or have a conversation with the bride's family about whether they'd like to do the honors. Any combination of hosts is fine—the groom's parents, the couple, the bride's parents, or any or all of the above.

When making a decision about hosting, particularly in regard to who's paying for what, it's best to be honest and straightforward about budgets and expectations and to be respectful of people's limitations. Keep in mind that compromise is often the key here and that the goal should always be a good time for everyone.

who's invited?

Having been born out of the actual wedding rehearsal, the dinner typically is only for those people who are actually participating in the ceremony, in addition to the couple's parents and grandparents. The usual suspects are

- The bride and groom
- Members of the wedding party
- The officiant
- The siblings and parents of the bride and groom

In addition, if the bride and/or groom have stepparents, they are invited with their spouses. (Generally, no one should ever be seated at the same table as their ex-spouses.) The wedding party's spouses, fiancé(e)s, and live-in companions should also be invited. If an attendant has a guest who doesn't fit this bill, while *technically* they don't have to be invited, it's considerate to include them as well.

Any children of the bride or groom from a previous marriage usually attend as well, unless they are too young. Junior bridesmaids and ushers, flower girls, and ring bearers may also be invited if the hour isn't too late. After that, any number of people may be invited—though it's completely optional. While not required, the most common additions to the group are godparents, aunts and uncles, nephews and nieces, cousins, and close friends.

ask anna: *who* requests the pleasure of your company?

Q: *If both families are covering the cost of the rehearsal dinner, whose names go on the invitation?*

anna: The invitation should be issued by those who are paying the bill, so the answer is: both families. As to who is listed first, it really doesn't matter. If the couple is paying, they might (if they want) still choose to have their parents listed as the honorary hosts.

The View From Afar. Given that the groom's family frequently is not from the same town as the bride's, rehearsal dinners are most often held at restaurants, clubs, or private dining rooms at hotels rather than at a private home. The bride's family can be a big help in giving ideas about suitable venues. Also, when planning from a distance, it's easy for little details to get away from you, so be sure to check on things such as

* Is there someone in town, such as the bride or her mother or sister, who can be a go-to person for help? (If the rehearsal dinner venue has a caterer or event planner, they can be an invaluable resource for keeping track of everything on-site and contacting local vendors in advance.)

* Dinner can be plated or a buffet, but if the host can't be there to sample the menu, be sure to use a local contact to test things out before ordering.

* Flowers—do you want them, and will the venue supply them or do you need to ask the bride's family for the name of a local florist?

* Don't forget to consider seating charts and arrange for place cards, if you plan on using them.

ask anna: what's the official word on inviting the officiant?

Q: *Do we really have to invite our wedding officiant to the rehearsal dinner? We hardly know him.*

anna: Yes. If nothing else, you'll be much more comfortable with him or her the next day, having spent time socializing. Remember, too, that this person is joining you—for life—to your true love. Returning the favor with a nice dinner isn't a bad way to say "thank you."

Gifts at the Rehearsal Dinner. There is no obligation to give gifts at the rehearsal dinner. However, this time is often used to exchange gifts between the couple and their attendants, as well as any gifts that the couple and their family members might be planning to exchange. (For more, see Chapter 9, "All About Party Gifts—and Those All-Important Thank-Yous," page 111.)

Who Toasts? Toasts are made during dinner or dessert. The host—often the groom's father—makes the first toast, welcoming the guests and saluting the forthcoming marriage. He is generally followed by the bride's father, and then by attendants and anyone else who wishes to say something. Sometimes the bride and groom stand and speak about each other; they might end by proposing a toast first to their respective parents and then to all their friends and relatives in attendance. (For more, see Chapter 11, "Cheers! Making Toasts," page 139.)

Caution: Don't Get Carried Away. Let's face it, there's hardly anything less fun than a hangover. But a hangover on your wedding day? That won't do at all! Even if makeup can cover the bleary eyes and dry skin, a queasy stomach and pounding headache are hardly how you want to experience your big day. It's easy to get carried away, as the rehearsal dinner is the big kickoff to all the fun; just remember to save some of your energy for the next day—and night!

the big day
receptions

While enjoyable and memorable in their own right, all of the parties that we've discussed so far are really just a prelude to *the* party. The **wedding reception** is not only the biggest celebration of the wedding but also the one that usually most reflects the couple's taste and personality.

THE RECEPTION:
A Party That Lasts a Lifetime

There are several reasons why wedding receptions linger in people's memories long after other parties have been forgotten: First and foremost, a reception is a celebration of the wedding ceremony that precedes it, in which two people have publicly declared their desire to spend the rest of their lives together. In addition, a reception brings together extended family—many of whom may not have seen each other in some time—along with a unique cross-section of the bride and groom's friends. These factors alone are enough to set a wedding celebration apart, but a successful reception is also a party like no other—an event designed to cheer guests' hearts, souls, and senses and to create a lasting bond among everyone who attends.

One of my favorite receptions was a fall wedding outside in the mountains. The afternoon air was chilly, and we were greeted with warm spiced apple cider when we arrived. The wedding was small, and the ceremony was fairly short, taking place beside a small pond. Afterward we enjoyed hors d'oeuvres of local cheeses, fruits, and nuts while we mingled and admired the spectacular views of the foliage. For dinner, we went into a warm and cozy tent for butternut squash soup and duck. The hit of the party however, was the mashed potato station, where mashed potatoes were served in martini glasses with all the fixings anyone could possibly want. Everyone loved it—well, except for the one poor little boy who, on taking his first bite, was so very disappointed to realize it wasn't ice cream!

party timeline

Most weddings are followed by a reception that day, either immediately or within a few hours. (For wedding receptions held on a different day than the wedding, see "Belated Receptions," page 64.)

A wedding reception involves many more moving parts than the average party does. Not only will you need to provide food and drink for all of your guests, but the typical reception also includes flowers, musical entertainment, a photographer and/or videographer, and transportation for the wedding party and close family. And then there are all those special touches, such as the wedding cake, the receiving line, toasts and first dances, the tossing of the bouquet, and so on.

If this sounds like it involves a lot of planning, you're right. Before you start to panic, however, bear in mind one piece of advice: The earlier you get started in your planning, the easier it will be to bring all of these elements together into a beautiful—and stress-free—wedding day.

In particular, wedding experts agree that you should try to pin down your reception site at least nine months ahead of time, if possible. Once your venue is set, you can then begin putting all of the other pieces into place, including hiring your various service providers, and finalizing the food and entertainment.

Assuming a full year between the engagement and the wedding, here's a quick overview of what should happen when (if your engagement length is different, simply adjust as needed):

9 to 12 months in advance:

- Select your wedding date
- Choose the style of the reception you want
- Pick a reception site
- Determine your budget
- Begin developing a master guest list
- Decide if you want to use a wedding consultant to help plan the reception
- If you do decide to use a consultant, begin interviewing candidates
- If necessary, interview and begin selecting a florist, a photographer/videographer, musical entertainment, and/or a caterer

6 to 9 months in advance:

- ✳ Finalize your guest list

- ✳ Order invitations, and send out save-the-date cards

- ✳ Reserve accommodations for out-of-town guests

- ✳ Choose the reception menu and type of food and beverage service

- ✳ Discuss ideas for floral arrangements with the florist

- ✳ Discuss ideas for reception set list with the band or DJ

- ✳ Begin planning the rehearsal dinner and any post-wedding parties

3 to 6 months in advance:

- ✳ Finalize all plans for the reception, rehearsal dinner, and post-wedding parties

2 months in advance:

- ✳ Send out wedding invitations

who hosts?

The wedding reception is traditionally hosted by the bride's parents. Until recently, it was also the accepted custom that the bride's parents would *pay* for the entire reception as well. These days, this custom has given way to financial reality. While the bride's parents often still pick up much of the reception costs, surveys have found that only a fraction of weddings are now paid for exclusively by the bride's family. In most cases, contributions are also made by the groom's parents and by the couple themselves. Who is willing to chip in on the reception—and how much they're willing to spend—is a subject that should be broached early in the planning process. This will allow you to move ahead with a clear idea of your budget parameters. (For more tips on navigating finances, see Chapter 6, "Dollars and Sense: Planning for Success," page 69.)

If the groom's parents are paying for a substantial amount of the reception expenses, then the parents of the bride and the groom may choose to co-host the wedding, with both sets of names appearing on the wedding invitation. Alternatively, if the couple is paying for the entire wedding, they may decide to list only their own names on the invitations as hosts.

who's invited?

Since serving food and drinks to your guests typically accounts for about half the cost of a reception, the bigger your guest list is, the more expensive the reception is likely to be. With that in mind, the engaged couple and their parents will need to come up with an estimate of how many people in total they plan to invite. They each then need to come up with their own partial guest lists, which will be combined into the master guest list.

In drawing up these guest lists, the best approach is to start by listing your "must-have" guests—family members and close friends you wouldn't dream of not inviting. Next, create a second list of "hopefuls"—guests you'd like to invite, if space allows. As your budget and guest list begin to solidify, you can then start to decide which of your hopefuls you'll be able to invite.

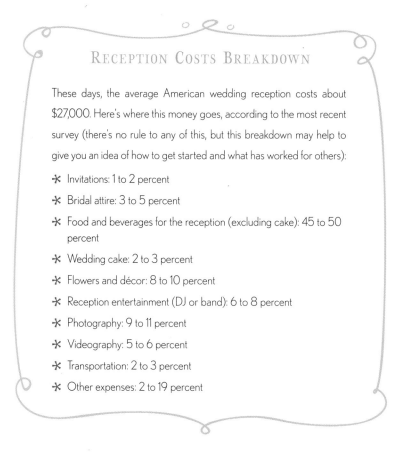

RECEPTION COSTS BREAKDOWN

These days, the average American wedding reception costs about $27,000. Here's where this money goes, according to the most recent survey (there's no rule to any of this, but this breakdown may help to give you an idea of how to get started and what has worked for others):

* Invitations: 1 to 2 percent
* Bridal attire: 3 to 5 percent
* Food and beverages for the reception (excluding cake): 45 to 50 percent
* Wedding cake: 2 to 3 percent
* Flowers and décor: 8 to 10 percent
* Reception entertainment (DJ or band): 6 to 8 percent
* Photography: 9 to 11 percent
* Videography: 5 to 6 percent
* Transportation: 2 to 3 percent
* Other expenses: 2 to 19 percent

Two Ways to Divide Up the Guest List. How you divvy up your guest list is obviously your own business, but most couples and their parents do it in one of two ways:

* They divide the list into equal parts, with the bride and groom, the bride's parents, and the groom's parents each inviting one-third of the guests.
* The bride and groom reserve half the list for themselves, with the other half of the list divided equally between the two sets of parents.

ask anna: can I wait to invite "standby" guests?

Q: *Can we invite our guests in "tiers," starting with those we really want there, and then sending out more invitations as regrets come back?*

anna: A standby guest list is a risky proposition, since it creates the potential for hurt feelings or for guests to feel slighted. I'm hesitant to encourage you to go down this road, but I do understand the realities of controlling your guest list and budget. If at all possible, invite the entire list at the same time (typically, 10 to 20 percent of invited guests will send regrets). If you do choose to send invitations to a standby list, be very discreet. Guests must not have even the slightest idea that they're not your first choice. Your first wave of invitations should be mailed at least two months before the wedding. Allow a minimum of four weeks for the first set of guests to reply before sending invitations to your standby list; then be sure the second group of invitees also has at least four weeks' advance notice of the wedding so that they have time to respond and make travel arrangements.

wedding gifts

All invited guests are expected to give a wedding gift to the bride and groom—including guests who have been invited but can't attend the wedding. Guests can send their gifts to the couple anytime after they receive the invitation, or they can bring a gift to the wedding reception. As for how late you can send a wedding gift, the "one-year rule" is a myth—if for any reason you haven't given the couple a gift by the time the wedding is over, just send one as soon as you can—better late than never. Another myth I'd like to dispel for good is that your wedding gift should be equal in value to the cost of your dinner. Not true! When considering how much to spend on your wedding gift, your budget and your relationship to the couple should be the determining factors.

Unopened wedding gifts may be displayed at the reception if you wish, but they should always be opened in private. (For a detailed discussion of wedding gifts, see Chapter 9, "All About Party Gifts—and Those All-Important Thank-Yous," page 111.)

SELECTING A RECEPTION SITE

In planning a wedding reception, the most important decision you'll make is where to hold the event. The town you select will dictate who will be traveling to the wedding and how far they'll have to come, as well as their choice of accommodations once they arrive. The site you choose will set the tone for the wedding in terms of ambience and will also influence the way the party itself unfolds—particularly if the reception site has its own caterer and/or events planner.

As mentioned above, it's important to reserve your chosen reception site as early as possible—*especially* if (1) the spot you have in mind is a popular venue for weddings and (2) you're getting married at a popular time of year, such as late spring. When inquiring about a venue that's in high demand, you can improve your chances by having several possible wedding dates in mind—for example, three consecutive weekends that might work for you.

types of venues

Once you've determined the town or city where the reception will take place, you'll need to decide on a venue. The one that's right for you will depend on how you envision your own big day.

WHAT VENUE IS RIGHT FOR YOU?

type of venue	pros and cons
Restaurant	Built-in food, service, and cleanup; space considerations may limit number of guests and size of dance floor
Hotel	Likely to have experience hosting weddings, and may also offer cost-saving wedding packages; settings can be bland
Club	An elegant way to go; check to see if you can bring a caterer—private clubs can vary in the quality of their food service
Private home	Unmatched for intimacy; will require you to hire caterer and bring in tables, chairs, linens, and possibly a tent
Museum or gallery	Exotic setting makes for a stellar event; importing food and entertainment will take some planning
Garden	Natural surroundings create an unforgettable atmosphere; be sure to have a rainy-day backup site
Historic landmark	Who wouldn't like to host a reception in your own mansion-for-a-day? Very old buildings may have limited kitchen facilities and electrical supply
Beach	Romantic setting is hard to beat; logistical challenges rise in proportion to your distance from civilization

five things you should know before reserving your reception site

1. *Does the venue have a site manager or events planner?* If so, this person will be responsible for coordinating everything that happens at the reception. If the site handles a lot of weddings, the manager is likely to have a lot of experience making sure receptions go smoothly—a huge plus.

2. *Does the site have its own in-house catering service?* The presence of an in-house caterer has its good points and sometimes not-so-good points. The upside: It saves you the trouble of finding a caterer yourself and ensures that everything needed for feeding your guests, from stoves to table linens, will be on the premises. The potential downside: Rather than being able to select a caterer of your own choosing, you're stuck with that caterer's offerings, for better or worse—so be sure to taste the menu before you commit.

3. *What's the maximum seating capacity for the venue?* If it's less than the number on your guest list, you've got problems.

4. *Are there any restrictions on décor (including flowers), photography and videography, and/or the type of music that can be played?* For example, some sites don't allow amplified instruments, and others require a rented dance floor so their own floor won't be scratched.

5. *Will the site allow you to bring in your own liquor?* Purchasing your own alcohol can often be a way to save substantially on beverage costs.

Putting Together Your Reception Team. Receptions typically involve a team of service providers, including a florist, caterer, photographer and/or videographer, musical entertainment, and limousine company. If the reception site has a manager or events planner, he or she will be a key part of the team. If you decide to hire a wedding consultant (also known as a wedding planner), he or she will likely take a lead role in helping to hire and direct the other members of your team. (For more details on working with service providers, see Chapter 7, "Food, Flowers, and Other Fun Stuff," page 79.)

As noted in the "Party Timeline" section (see page 44), you should start interviewing and selecting your service providers at least nine months before the wedding date, if possible—both to ensure that the vendors you want will be available on the day of the wedding and to allow everyone plenty of prep time.

feeding the multitudes

In any wedding reception, food plays a major part. There's no such thing as a traditional wedding menu—in fact, this is a fabulous opportunity to put the couple's personal tastes on display, both through creative menu choices and innovative presentation. How you serve the food will depend in part on how formal you want the reception to be. There are basically three ways to go: A **plated meal**—the most formal option—where guests are seated and waiters bring around the various courses; a somewhat less-formal **buffet meal**, in which guests get their own food from a buffet table or from several food stations, each featuring different selections (an increasingly popular option, since it avoids the crush of a buffet line); or **passed-tray service**, in which waiters circulate with trays of hors d'oeuvres (this is typically done during the cocktail hour prior to dinner—though some weddings feature only a cocktail reception, with no meal).

HAVE YOUR CAKE AND EAT IT, TOO.

You're vanilla. He's chocolate. You fall in love, you get engaged. . . . You have to pick a wedding cake. Ah, sweet compromise. Many guys might pass on picking flowers and invitations, but the cakes tend to get their attention. One way to go is to have a wedding cake with different flavored layers and fillings to make everyone happy. Also popular: Get your own cake. Brides are often choosing the wedding cake and letting the grooms have what *they* want at the rehearsal dinner. And of course there's also the regional tradition of groom's cakes—a smaller cake decorated to showcase the groom's interests.

SIX KEY MOMENTS IN EVERY RECEPTION

1. **The receiving line.** Let's start by setting the record straight: A receiving line is not required. However, the bride and groom *do* have to thank each and every one of their guests for coming to their wedding—and a receiving line really is the best way to be sure that they don't miss anyone, especially if the wedding is large (more than 75 people). A receiving line is also a great (and efficient) way to be sure that all the guests have a chance to meet the couple's parents and attendants. The receiving line is held either at the ceremony site as people exit after the service or as soon as the couple reaches the reception site. It usually includes (in order) the bride's parents (mother first), the groom's parents, the bride and groom, the maid or matron of honor, and the bride's attendants. If the wedding party is small, the best man and groomsmen may join as well, though flower girls and ring bearers are not included. Thoughtful tip: When the receiving line is held at the reception site, have a waiter offer drinks to those waiting, and have a small table where guests can place their drinks while going through the line.

2. **The best man's toast.** Traditionally, this occurs as soon as the champagne is poured—which in turn happens as soon as everyone is seated, if the reception is a sit-down dinner, or as soon as everyone enters the reception, if it's a cocktail buffet. The best man then gets the guests' attention, and offers the first toast. While no other toasts are required, additional toasts are always encouraged. It's not uncommon for the maid/matron of honor and the fathers of the bride and groom to follow with toasts of their own, welcoming the guests and saluting the newly married couple. (For more details, see Chapter 11, "Cheers! Making Toasts," page 139.)

3. **The first dance.** It's customary for the bride and groom to dance the first dance of the reception together, while the guests watch and applaud. There may also be special dances reserved for the bride and her father, the groom and his mother, and the wedding party. (See "May I Have This Dance?" page 55.)

MAY I HAVE THIS DANCE?

What girl doesn't blush a little at those words? From the couple's first steps onto the dance floor to the last song of the night, here are some ideas to help create the perfect soundtrack for the evening:

First Dance (Bride and Groom)
Can't Help Falling In Love (Elvis Presley)
At Last (Etta James)
Wonderful Tonight (Eric Clapton)
When You Say Nothing At All (Allison Krauss)
Amazed (Lonestar)

Second Dance (Bride and Her Father)
My Girl (Temptations)
Unforgettable (Natalie Cole)
Isn't She Lovely? (Stevie Wonder)
You Are So Beautiful (Joe Cocker)
The Way You Look Tonight (Frank Sinatra)

Third Dance (Groom and His Mother)
Moon River (Andy Williams)
Stand By Me (Ben E. King)
Have I Told You Lately (Rod Stewart)
Fly Me to the Moon (Frank Sinatra)
Just the Way You Are (Billy Joel)

Fourth Dance (Bridal Party)
That's What Friends Are For (Dionne Warwick)
We Are Family (Sly and the Family Stone)
Celebration (Kool & the Gang)
You Sexy Thing (Hot Chocolate)
You're My Best Friend (Queen)

Last Dance
Last Dance (Donna Summer)
(I've Had) the Time of My Life (Bill Medley/Jennifer Warnes)
What a Wonderful World (Louis Armstrong)
Can You Feel the Love Tonight? (Elton John)
As Time Goes By (Jimmy Durante)

ask anna: what to do about wallflowers?

Q: *I know that not everyone at my reception will dance, but how can I encourage people to at least get up from their tables after dinner and mingle?*

anna: If guests want to linger over coffee and dessert at their tables, that really is okay. But I do love the idea of putting some chairs, benches, or ottomans around the edge of the dance floor, so that people can feel a little more included in the dancing, even if they aren't kicking up their heels themselves. Just be sure to leave a little room between them and the dance floor!

4. **The cutting of the cake.** This happens at the end of the entrée course (if the reception is a sit-down dinner). The band leader or DJ will typically announce the cake-cutting, at which point the bride and groom walk over to the cake table (or the cake is wheeled out from the kitchen). The bride places her hand on the knife handle and the groom places his hand over hers, and they cut off a small piece of cake, which is placed on a waiting plate with two forks. The groom feeds the bride the first bite, she feeds him the second, and they kiss. (Please: no smashing the cake into each other's faces—it's so tacky, and the last thing the bride wants to worry about is fixing her lip gloss again!) One of the waitstaff then cuts the rest of the cake and serves it to the guests.

5. **The tossing of the bouquet.** This is traditionally done just before the bride and groom leave the reception. All the single females gather on the dance floor, and then the bride turns her back to the group and tosses her bouquet over her head to the waiting women. (Since many brides want to keep the bouquet they carried down the aisle, the florist will typically make a special "tossing bouquet" for just this purpose.) Supposedly, she who catches the bouquet will be the next to marry—which is why you'll often see as many women dodging the flying flowers as rushing to catch them!

6. **The send-off for the bride and groom.** At the end of the reception, the bride and groom will often be sent on their way with a formal farewell from the guests. The bride's and groom's attendants and the other guests form a corridor, and the couple dashes through it into a waiting car or limo, while being showered with birdseed, rose petals, soap bubbles, or any other acceptably biodegradable material. (The traditional handfuls of rice have been banished because rice makes walkways too slippery.) The car—or the boat—then carries the happy couple away. At the end of one wedding reception I attended that was held at a yacht club, the couple left from the dock on a beautiful old wooden launch. So glamorous!

Lucky Number Seven.... And there's a seventh moment that can occur at any wedding reception: The moment when something goes wrong. The sprinklers on the lawn turn on. The band is late. The generators fail. These things will happen. And the best thing you can do is just go with it and laugh—you'll enjoy yourself more, and it will help set the tone for your guests until the lights come on, the music starts playing, and your shoes dry off.

SIMPLE COMFORTS

I recently attended an outdoor lakeside wedding on the most beautiful summer day. Perfect—except that I'm very pale and had forgotten sunscreen (a must for me), and there was no shade to be had anywhere. What I wouldn't have given for a bottle of SPF 15! The mistake was mine, but it brings up an important point: namely, that seeing to guests' comfort goes beyond keeping their drinks full. Think about any needs your guests might not have anticipated or little extras they might be grateful for. At a summer wedding party, bottles of water, sunscreen, paper fans (you can even dress them up with quotations or pictures of the couple) or inexpensive Chinese parasols all make welcome additions. (If the party is at the beach, consider providing basic flip-flops to keep barefoot guests from scorching their feet.) For winter parties, have a clean path cleared to the door and hot cocoa or cider waiting to warm up guests coming in from the cold. A little thoughtfulness will leave a lasting impression!

IMPROMPTU AFTER-PARTY
DO'S AND DON'TS

No one wants a fabulous party to draw to a close, and many wedding receptions end with all the guests—and sometimes even the newly married couple—carrying the party on to a fresh location, often at a hotel the guests are using, a bar or restaurant, or one of the guests' homes. At one terrific after-party I went to, we were in the unique (and lucky!) position of having a bed and breakfast all to ourselves, so we didn't have to worry about bothering any other guests. The staff had been forewarned that it might be a late night and weren't expected to be on hand. We brought over some extra food from the reception, and we played music on the stereo and danced until the early hours of the morning.

Sometimes guests even stay at the reception location—just be absolutely sure that it's okay with the staff, so that you won't be in the way of any cleaning up. A few more do's and don'ts to consider:

- Do be considerate when putting the word out to the other guests. After all, no one wants to feel excluded from the fun and leave the reception on a sour note.

- Don't cut the wedding reception short just to meet people for an after-party.

- Do make sure there is a designated driver or take taxis if you're going to another location.

- If you're heading to a bar or restaurant on a whim, do call and be sure they will be open.

- Don't worry if you're just too tired to make an appearance; these parties are only for a little extra fun.

but wait—there's more!

farewell brunches and belated receptions

The vows have been recited, the toasts have been made, the cake has been cut, and the bride and groom have been sent on their way. What a shame it's all over!

Or is it? These days it's becoming increasingly popular to extend the wedding celebration past the reception itself, in the form of a **farewell brunch**, held the morning after the reception. And if the situation calls for it, a **belated reception** is the perfect way for the bride and groom to celebrate with friends and family who weren't able to attend the wedding.

THE FAREWELL BRUNCH

A brunch on the morning after a wedding reception is a wonderful way for guests to get together one last time to enjoy each other's company while having some good food and coffee before heading back home.

With the formality of the ceremony and reception safely behind them, the key words for both hosts and guests at this event are *informality* and *inclusiveness*. The brunch typically is open to everyone who attended the wedding, but it should be made clear that attendance is purely optional—this is a convenience. The brunch should also have a relatively late start time—since some guests may be sleeping in—and a flexible serving schedule, so that guests who have to leave promptly to catch a plane or begin a long drive can eat and be on their way. A buffet-style brunch is ideal, since it allows people to eat at various times without inconveniencing anyone else. If the brunch is held in a restaurant that doesn't feature a buffet, make it clear to the restaurant that people will most likely be arriving and placing their brunch orders at different times.

party timeline

This brunch is held the day after the reception, starting anywhere from early morning to early afternoon.

who hosts?

The farewell brunch is traditionally hosted by the parents of the bride, either at their home or at a restaurant or private room in a hotel, as an extension of the wedding reception. There's no hard and fast rule about this, however, and the brunch can really be hosted by anyone. Another popular approach is for a close friend or relative of the bride's family to offer to host the brunch in their home, often as a wedding gift to the couple.

Another alternative is to have multiple hosts—such as the parents of the bride and groom, the attendants, friends of the couple, or any combination thereof. This allows the various hosts to split the cost of what can end up being a rather expensive undertaking, especially if the brunch is a catered affair or is being hosted at an upscale restaurant.

who's invited?

As mentioned above, in the typical farewell brunch, printed or handwritten invitations are extended to all wedding guests at the same time wedding invitations are sent, to allow time to coordinate travel. Theoretically, this means the brunch could draw a crowd as big as the wedding itself, which could make for a less-than-intimate experience, to say the least. In practice, however, only a portion of the wedding guests—usually those who have either traveled a distance and stayed over for the night, or who live right in town—will end up attending, keeping the event to a manageable size.

Another approach is to limit the brunch to a smaller circle—for example, the parents of the bride and groom, the wedding party, and close relatives. This has the advantage of maximizing intimacy while minimizing expenses—but whoever is hosting the brunch will need to consider whether these benefits are really worth excluding the relatively small number of additional guests who might otherwise attend.

WHERE ARE THE LOVEBIRDS?

The bride and groom may or may not attend the farewell brunch, depending on their travel plans and their inclinations. Obviously, the brunch guests would enjoy the opportunity to mingle and chat with the newly married couple. But as stated earlier, this party is purely optional. If the couple is already winging their way to an exotic locale—or even if they haven't left town yet but prefer to sleep in and order their breakfast from room service—that's perfectly okay.

tranquility base—choosing a brunch venue

When deciding where to host a brunch, think *calm* and *tranquil*. Chances are, the wedding has provided guests with plenty of excitement. The farewell brunch should be a warm, relaxed, unhurried gathering, and the setting should encourage this:

- ✳ In warm-weather months, a brunch outside on a restaurant terrace, in a formal garden, or on tables set up in a backyard can provide a wonderful final scene for a wedding, ideally with chirping birds providing a backdrop to the murmur of conversation and the soft clinking of tableware.

- ✳ A private room or quiet corner of a restaurant or hotel dining room lets guests gather in a setting conducive to mingling, while also ensuring maximum flexibility in food service.

- ✳ A brunch in a private home is unbeatable in terms of intimacy, but feeding everyone in this setting can be a challenge. If you go this route, consider using a caterer.

- ✳ For a more casual brunch, consider serving a Continental breakfast—with pitchers of fresh-squeezed orange juice, baskets of muffins and croissants, bagels and cream cheese, fresh fruit, and a variety of coffees and teas.

BELATED RECEPTIONS

If the wedding is very small or was held at a destination that precluded many people from attending, or if the couple was unable to hold a reception—because they eloped, for example, or had to report to military service immediately after the ceremony—then the couple and/or their parents may decide to throw a belated reception to celebrate the marriage. This event can be as formal or informal as the couple and their hosts choose to make it. Some belated receptions are structured around a casual cocktail buffet or barbecue, while others may mirror an actual wedding reception, right down to the cutting of the cake. The one way in which belated receptions *always* differ from the real thing is that wedding gifts are not expected (unless a guest was invited to the wedding itself and has not

given a gift yet)—although close friends and relatives are certainly free to give gifts if they choose. (For more on wedding gifts, see Chapter 9, "All About Party Gifts—and Those All-Important Thank-Yous," page 111.)

party timeline

Belated receptions can be held several days, weeks, or even months after the wedding ceremony. Invitations can be printed or written on fill-in cards and should be mailed out four to six weeks in advance.

who hosts?

A belated reception can be hosted by the bride's parents, the groom's parents, the couple themselves—or any other family member or close friend.

who's invited?

Basically, the hosts and the couple can invite anyone they want to. Because belated receptions are often less elaborate (and thus less expensive) than a regular reception, the guest list can often be expanded to include those who might not ordinarily have been invited to the wedding itself.

Destination Reception

Celebrating an exotic destination wedding after the fact? Here are some ways to bring your wedding to your reception guests back home:

Save-the-date cards. Buy postcards at the wedding destination to send as save-the-date cards for the reception.

Invitations. Incorporate colors from the landscape where the wedding is being held—or, if the wedding has already taken place when invitations are mailed, a photo from the wedding ceremony.

Photos. In addition to the usual slideshows and videos, have a couple of wedding photos blown up and displayed—or use glass-topped tables for the reception, and place photos from the wedding underneath the glass for guests to look at during dinner.

Food. Bring in elements of the local cuisine from the place of your wedding. If you're worried the food may be too exotic for everyone, incorporate elements into just the hors d'oeuvres or the dessert.

Music. Choose local music from the place where your wedding was held.

Flowers. Use flowers native to the wedding locale. If that's too expensive, use them as accents in your arrangements, or simply tuck a few in the bride's hair.

Party favors. Bring back tokens from your trip, such as candied fruits or nuts, teas, or local handicrafts.

belated reception basics

If the couple had no reception at all after their ceremony—or a very small one—then a belated reception may have all the features of a regular reception, including a receiving line, toasts, a wedding cake, and musical entertainment and dancing. If the bride wishes, she may even wear her wedding dress again (see "Ask Anna: Is It Okay to Wear My Bridal Gown a Month after the Wedding?" page 68). As mentioned above, the only significant difference is that guests are not expected to give the couple gifts. If family members or close friends want to give wedding gifts anyway, that's fine—but these should be presented to the couple in private, to avoid causing discomfort to guests who didn't bring a gift. For the same reason, gifts should *never* be displayed at a belated reception.

SECOND RECEPTIONS

If the couple did have a full-blown reception after their wedding but got married in a place that prevented a number of family members or friends from attending—for instance, if the wedding was held in the bride's hometown, which is located far away from where most of the groom's family and friends reside—then the couple or their family may choose to have a second wedding celebration in the weeks following the wedding, held in a place convenient to those who didn't attend the actual wedding. My friends Ken and Jessica did this. They married and held a reception in her hometown in western New York, but many members of Ken's family couldn't attend, since they live in Hawaii. As a compromise, they held a second reception two weeks later in Hawaii while on their honeymoon, so they could celebrate with his extended family as well.

In cases like theirs, where the couple has already had a reception, these types of second receptions should not mirror the wedding reception. Instead, they tend to be on the less formal side—a cocktail party, brunch, buffet dinner, or barbecue, for example—with invitations sent out two to four weeks in advance. There is no wedding cake or receiving line—though the couple should stand by the door along with the host and hostess to greet all arrivals and introduce themselves. Attendance by members of the wedding party is purely optional, as are wedding gifts.

ask anna: is it okay to wear my bridal gown a month after the wedding?

Q: My in-laws are having a post-reception party in my husband's hometown, and they are eager to have me wear my wedding gown. Would this really be appropriate? Our wedding was over a month ago.

anna: It *would* be a bit much to wear your wedding gown for the entire party. On the other hand, if you and your parents-in-law would like your guests to see what you look like in your gown, it's perfectly okay to wear it at the start of the celebration, while guests are arriving. Once everyone's had a chance to see you, you can switch into regular party clothes for the remainder of the event.

chapter six

dollars and sense

planning for success

No matter what kind of wedding party you're throwing, from a casual engagement party to a Jack and Jill shower to a formal reception, there are some planning tips that apply across the board. These include **timing guidelines**, suggestions for dealing with **budgets and finances**, and a few other **key details** you want to be sure not to overlook.

BUDGETING YOUR TIME AND MONEY

Behind every great wedding party are a detailed plan and a careful budget. Here are some tips on how to stay on top of your party planning and how to navigate some potentially sticky financial conversations.

timing, timing, timing

When it comes to planning, there are two big essentials: First, make sure that you book your venue and your service providers far enough in advance to get the locations and professionals you want—*especially* for the reception! Second, make sure that you stay far enough ahead of the game to be able to *enjoy* the parties themselves.

WEDDING PARTY PLANNING TIMELINE

An event-by-event guide on how far in advance to...

EVENT	RESERVE THE VENUE	HIRE SERVICE PROVIDERS	SEND OUT INVITATIONS
Engagement party	At least one month	Three to six weeks*	Three to six weeks*
Shower	One to three months*	One to two months *	One month
(Bachelor)ette party	Three to eight weeks*	Three weeks	One to three months**
Rehearsal dinner	One to six months*	One to three months*	Four to six weeks
Farewell brunch	Three to six months	Six to eight weeks	Six to eight weeks
Belated reception	One to three months*	One to three months*	Four to six weeks

* Less time for a small or informal party; more time for a large or formal party
** More time for a party involving plane and hotel reservations

selecting a venue and service providers

If possible, a reception site should be nailed down nine to twelve months before the wedding date. Ideally, you should also have settled on your caterer, florist, musicians, photographer, and other service providers—and be actively discussing your plans with them—at least six months before the wedding. (See the reception "Party Timeline," page 44.)

Since the other wedding parties in this book generally involve smaller guest lists and venues, tend to be less demanding in terms of specifics (such as a full kitchen, dance floor, and room for a band), and don't involve as many service providers, you won't need quite as much advance time when you plan them. But that doesn't give you license to slack off!

money matters

Budgets and money can be very touchy subjects, especially since the costs involved in a wedding and the social events surrounding it can quickly reach astronomical proportions. Here are some of the realities about how people are budgeting for their weddings these days, and some tips on how to broach the potential sticky subject of sharing expenses.

Who Pays for What: Traditions and Modern Realities. In the not-so-distant past, the bride's family traditionally paid for the engagement party, the wedding and reception, a brunch the next day, and a belated reception (if there was one). The groom's family financed the rehearsal dinner and the groom himself covered the honeymoon, while shower costs were paid for by the host (usually a close friend or relative).

While there's nothing wrong with following these traditions, the reality is that this isn't always possible anymore. The reasons why don't matter; what *does* matter is that people need to know it's perfectly okay to make other arrangements. The important thing is to talk over these arrangements—and how you all plan on sharing the financial burden—as early in the planning process as possible.

* The *engagement party* is generally paid for by the hosts. If the bride and groom are throwing their own party, they cover the expenses, though their parents and/or friends may offer to help defray the costs.

* *Showers and (bachelor)ette parties* are fairly straightforward: Shower hosts are responsible for the event's costs. At (bachelor)ette parties, everyone usually covers themselves, plus a little extra to treat the bride or groom—although these arrangements should be discussed when the party is first being planned.

* When it comes to expenses, the wedding weekend, made up of the *rehearsal dinner, reception,* and *post-wedding brunch,* is the 800-pound gorilla. As I noted in Chapter 4 (see "Reception Costs Breakdown" page 48), the average cost of an American wedding reception these days is about $27,000. Add several thousand dollars for a rehearsal dinner, and some fraction of that for the farewell brunch, and you're talking real money—which is why it's important to talk about money right from the start.

so...let's talk

These financial conversations usually involve the main players in the wedding: the couple and their parents and/or stepparents (though siblings, aunts, and uncles may sometimes be involved as well). The first step is to find out who is willing to pay for what and how much everyone is able to contribute—which in turn will provide you with an overall budget to work with. You can then start making specific planning decisions from there.

The budget conversation can be initiated by any of the key participants: "Mom, Josh and I were hoping we could talk with you and Dad about our budget for the wedding," or "Kids, when you get a chance, we'd like to sit down and go over the budget for the wedding." It's important that everyone go into this conversation prepared. Know how much you can afford to contribute, and be realistic about your expectations. Once you're talking, remember to **be appreciative of any assistance, respectful of others' financial situations, honest about your own finances and expectations, and be willing to compromise.**

Remember, too, that it's okay if your initial budget is smaller than what you had in mind—there are *always* ways to cut corners without sacrificing quality. So keep your chin up: Emily Post's favorite wedding was one she attended at a humble country house where everything was simple and homemade but the day was full of love and laughter.

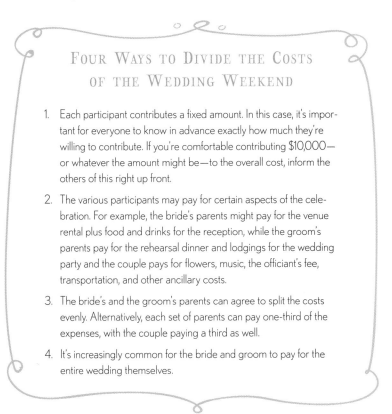

Four Ways to Divide the Costs of the Wedding Weekend

1. Each participant contributes a fixed amount. In this case, it's important for everyone to know in advance exactly how much they're willing to contribute. If you're comfortable contributing $10,000—or whatever the amount might be—to the overall cost, inform the others of this right up front.

2. The various participants may pay for certain aspects of the celebration. For example, the bride's parents might pay for the venue rental plus food and drinks for the reception, while the groom's parents pay for the rehearsal dinner and lodgings for the wedding party and the couple pays for flowers, music, the officiant's fee, transportation, and other ancillary costs.

3. The bride's and the groom's parents can agree to split the costs evenly. Alternatively, each set of parents can pay one-third of the expenses, with the couple paying a third as well.

4. It's increasingly common for the bride and groom to pay for the entire wedding themselves.

ask anna: who calls the shots?

Q: *My parents are paying for the entire wedding reception. Does that give them the final say on the big decisions, such as the venue, the caterer, and so on?*

anna: No. Let me say that again: no. Just because your parents are footing the bill doesn't mean they get to hold you hostage to their choices. Parents need to remember that the wedding day belongs to the couple. Although the parents are perfectly free to make suggestions, the specific decisions on locale, décor, food, and entertainment, and other details are ultimately up to the bride and groom.

At the same time, the couple needs to consider everyone's feelings in making their decisions. For any wedding party, it's important to select a venue and ambience that makes all of your guests comfortable.

There is one important exception to the "defer to the couple" rule: The bride and the groom absolutely must respect the budget limitations of whoever is paying for the event. If the parents who are footing the bill can see that the couple's choices are clearly exceeding the allotted amount, then it's time to step in firmly and remind them of their financial boundaries. When doing this, try to have a workable alternative or two at hand: "Jenny, I know you have your heart set on holding the reception at the Hale House, but the rental fee is simply more than we're able to spend. What about the country club or the Harborview Hotel? They're both beautiful, and they cost half the price."

If disagreements do arise, be prepared to discuss them calmly and always be open to compromise.

"LOVE EVERY IDEA FOR FIVE MINUTES"

I *adore* this concept. What does it mean? **Loving every idea for five minutes means giving people a chance to participate by voicing their opinions and allowing these opinions to be considered.**

For example, if the mother of the bride wants to offer her daughter her own bridal gown to wear down the aisle, allow her the chance to enjoy discussing this idea. The bride may well have her own thoughts about what dress she wants to wear, but by letting her mother talk out her idea, she's including her in the process—even if she doesn't choose to wear her mother's dress in the end: "Okay, Mom, I'll consider it. Why don't I go try it on with you?"

This way her mom gets to see and admire her daughter wearing her dress, while the bride is still free to say, "This is so beautiful, and thank you so much for offering it, but I really don't think it's what I had in mind." Or she might instead ask to use just part of the dress, such as the train or the veil. Regardless, the idea is to at least consider someone else's ideas. You don't have to make any promises—and, in fact, you shouldn't, unless you definitely plan to go with their suggestion, since that really would lead to hurt feelings.

This concept is a benevolent way to include others in your decision-making process without necessarily having to sacrifice your own ideas or vision. And who knows, you might even get a really great suggestion out of it!

Go Green!

Green just may be the new white in the world of weddings: From using recycled paper invitations to ordering organic flowers, there are endless ways to throw a beautiful party while also doing your part to help the environment. Here are a few ideas you might consider incorporating into your planning:

* Use invitations made with recycled paper. Look for paper manufactured from recycled or tree-free material, processed chlorine free (PCF), and printed with soy inks. Some even come with seeds for trees or wildflowers embedded in the grain of the paper, so guests can actually plant their invitations later!

* Hire a "green" wedding planner.

* Choose organic products wherever possible, from food and drinks to flowers. And be sure to send the flowers and extra food to a good home after the party, so they won't go to waste.

* Support local vendors—less energy will be used to transport goods, and the money you spend will go back into your own community.

* Skip the party favors, and let guests know that you've made a donation to a charity in their honor instead.

* Use biodegradable plates and utensils at the party—or, if you're using nondisposable items, wash them with biodegradable cleaners.

* When renting transportation for the wedding party, take advantage of the environmentally cleaner rental cars now being offered and rent a "luxury" car that's been converted to reduce emissions.

* Finally, "going green" can also mean cutting back on consumption altogether—which will save you money, too!

BACK TO BASICS

The devil, as they say, is in the details: Have you prepared for some of these easy-to-overlook party basics?

- ✳ **Directions:** Do your guests all have detailed directions for finding the venue, and a contact number in case they get lost?

- ✳ **Parking:** Do you need to post signs? Get permits or permissions? Arrange for valet services?

- ✳ **Coats:** Do you need a coat rack and hangers and/or a person to check guests' coats?

- ✳ **Powder rooms:** Are they clean and well stocked with soaps, fresh towels, and maybe flowers?

- ✳ **Babysitters:** Is a sitter needed, either for your own children or for those of your guests?

PARTY FAVORS: TOKENS OF AFFECTION

Party favors are little tokens that are handed out to guests. They're typically seen at receptions, though they may also be given out at engagement parties (often in the form of save-the-date reminders), showers, or (bachelor)ette parties. While thoughtful and entertaining, they are entirely optional. Usually inexpensive, they might range from bags of candy or cookies to paper fans or little matchboxes, and they almost always have the wedding date and the couple's names somewhere on them. Other popular ideas are small potted plants or packets of seeds, jars of jam or maple syrup, or even mini bottles of champagne (again, with personalized tags or labels). Anything is okay, so long as it fits in your budget and feels appropriate to your personality.

food, flowers,

and other fun stuff

When it comes to the special touches that make a wedding party—**flowers and other décor**, the **food**, perhaps some **music**, and a **photographer** and/or **videographer** to record it all—the first decision that you'll have to make is whether to **do it yourself** (perhaps with the help of family and friends) or **hire professional service providers** to do it for you. If your budget permits, the best approach often is to...

LEAVE IT TO THE PROS

Why hire a professional? In a word, experience. These guys do this all the time, and they do it well. Another reason is convenience: Hiring professionals (caterers, florists, pastry chefs, musicians, photographers, etc.) to help with your parties is often a great way to reduce your stress and add polish to your event. Of course, you don't just sign the check and disappear; it's important to stay closely involved in all aspects of the planning to be sure that your expectations are being met. Here are a few tips for working successfully with any of these party professionals:

Basic Advice for Working with Party Professionals. One of the best ways to choose service providers is to ask your friends for recommendations. There's no better testimonial than someone else's positive experience. A good friend will also be more likely to give you the most honest information.

- If at all possible, meet with all professionals in person before deciding to hire them. Call to set up an appointment rather than just dropping by their shop; this way you'll be sure to have their full attention. These professionals are often quite busy, and you may be interrupting them if you stop in unannounced.

- Look for someone you like and connect with. It's always easier to communicate your ideas to someone you relate well to. You'll be working closely with this person, and you want the experience to be fun!

- Know your budget for each service—including what's essential to you and what you can be flexible about.

- Ask to see samples of their work before agreeing to anything. It's essential to review portfolios, hear recordings of their music, or taste samples of their menus before signing them on. Also, be sure to check their references, even if they come recommended by a friend.

- Listen to their input and advice. These guys are the pros, after all, and their experience is part of what you're paying for (even when they are suggesting something contrary to your vision).

- Always have a written contract or agreement (see "Signing on the Dotted Line: Contracts," page 81).

- Discuss when and where any deliveries will take place. It's best if you or someone you designate can be on hand for all deliveries in case there are any problems.

- Ask for confirmation-call reminders, and be sure to provide accurate contact information, both for yourself and at least one backup person (in case you aren't available).

* Communicate on a regular basis, by phone or e-mail or in person, up to (and, if necessary, during) the event.

* After the event, be sure to thank them. Tipping is at your discretion and is usually reserved for service above and beyond the call of duty.

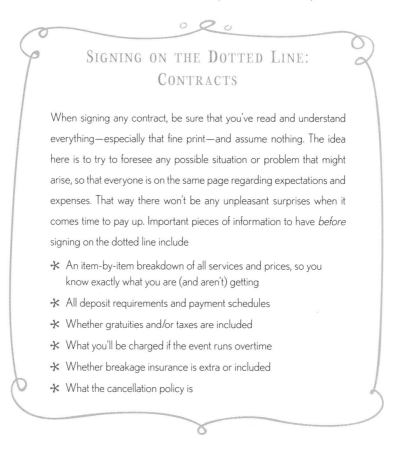

SIGNING ON THE DOTTED LINE: CONTRACTS

When signing any contract, be sure that you've read and understand everything—especially that fine print—and assume nothing. The idea here is to try to foresee any possible situation or problem that might arise, so that everyone is on the same page regarding expectations and expenses. That way there won't be any unpleasant surprises when it comes time to pay up. Important pieces of information to have *before* signing on the dotted line include

* An item-by-item breakdown of all services and prices, so you know exactly what you are (and aren't) getting
* All deposit requirements and payment schedules
* Whether gratuities and/or taxes are included
* What you'll be charged if the event runs overtime
* Whether breakage insurance is extra or included
* What the cancellation policy is

FOOD

Before you start to drool—I mean think—about what you want to serve, start by considering the big picture:

- What's your budget?
- How many people are you planning for?
- Where will the party be held?
- What time of day will it be?
- What kind of food service do you want?
- Think about the time of year and the location when planning your menu. (You'll save money by choosing foods that are local and/or in season.)
- Will you need help cooking or serving?
- If so, should you hire a caterer?

WHAT'S ON THE MENU?
A Venue-by-Venue Analysis

IF YOU GO WITH A PARTY AT...	THEN YOUR BEST BET IS...	SHOULD YOU HIRE A CATERER?
the classics		
Someone's home	Lots of options, from a seated brunch or dinner to a buffet to a cocktail party	Up to you
Country club	Seated brunch or dinner, with plated or buffet service	No need to worry
Favorite restaurant	Seated brunch or dinner with plated service	No need to worry
Best friend's place	Cake and champagne	Your choice, but probably not
relaxed and casual		
Park or beach	Casual picnic-style food and drinks	No
Site special to the couple, such as where they had their first date	Depends on the location. If a restaurant, then brunch or dinner. Otherwise, whatever is appropriate to the locale.	It depends on what you have in mind. See more below.
Backyard barbecue	Casual picnic-style food and drinks	Up to you
Bar for happy hour	Drinks and appetizers	No need to worry
reach for the stars		
Rent a boat for a cruise	Cocktails and hors d'oeuvres	Absolutely, if one doesn't come with the charter
Penthouse suite with a beautiful view	Drinks and a buffet dinner	Yes
Art gallery	Drinks and hors d'oeuvres	Yes—and you'll need their help serving, too

should you hire a caterer?

In general, hiring a caterer is a good idea whenever you have more than thirty guests. It will save you a lot of pre-party planning and prep time, and will free you up to focus on your guests during the party, rather than worry about getting the food ready. Many caterers can also provide servers if requested, and some will even agree to be on hand themselves for the event, to be sure things run smoothly in the kitchen.

working with a caterer

Start by thinking about your budget, and be upfront with the caterer about how much money you can spend. If you're firm about your budget, then it's the caterer's job to work within that figure. In addition

- Be sure to taste samples of any menu items you're considering. Also check to be sure the caterer and staff are professional in their appearance, attitude, and food preparation and presentation.

- Come prepared to discuss specific ideas or requests, and mention any likes or dislikes up front.

- Remember to be flexible and willing to consider the caterer's suggestions.

- Play to the caterer's strengths: Ask if they have a signature dish and what their most popular menu items are.

- Will the caterer be on hand for the party? Do they have staff that might be available to help serve and clean up? If so, can they visit the venue in advance?

Show Your Roots. No matter what kind of party you're throwing, you can easily add an infusion of your own particular culture. From the South? Have a barbecue, Southern style. From the East Coast? Go with a clambake (beach not required). A New Orleans native? *Laissez les bons temps rouler* with a Cajun-style feast! Northern Californian? Start with a vineyard inspiration and take things from there.

Your cultural statement can extend to the whole menu, or you can keep it to one item—such as letting your Texas roots shine through with some Shiner Bock beer or showing your Wisconsin pride with some featured local cheeses. I went to a great wedding in the Adirondacks where the rehearsal dinner was held in a cabin-type resort, with a picnic-style buffet of hamburgers, hot dogs, corn on the cob (one of Emily Post's favorite foods!), and coleslaw. Everyone had a wonderful time; the informality of finger foods made for a good icebreaker, and people had lots of opportunities to mingle in the buffet line and at unassigned tables.

BAR BASICS

Whether you hire a bartender or have guests fix their own drinks, there are a few basic items that every well-stocked bar should have:

- Lemon and lime slices
- Soft drinks (ginger ale, sodas, and possibly fruit juices)
- Beer, red and white wine, and champagne (if champagne toasts are planned)
- If hard liquor is being served: at least one bottle each of gin, vodka, scotch, bourbon, rum, and vermouth (if you're planning to offer martinis)
- Mixers (at least several bottles each of club soda or sparkling water and tonic water, plus a pitcher of plain water)
- Other mixers for specialty drinks (tomato juice and Tabasco sauce for Bloody Marys, orange juice for mimosas, cranberry juice and Cointreau for cosmopolitans, sour mix for whiskey sours, etc.)
- A jigger (for those who like to know exactly how much liquor they're pouring)
- A martini shaker for mixing drinks
- Plenty of ice

ask anna: should I hire a bartender?

Q: *My husband and I are hosting an engagement party for my son and his fiancée, and we're expecting about forty people. Do I need to hire a professional bartender?*

anna: Not necessarily. Many a fine party has been held at which guests are left to fix their own drinks. If you're expecting a large number of guests, however (and I'd say forty is pretty big), then hiring an experienced bartender makes a lot of sense. For one thing, a good bartender will know exactly what goes in the different drink recipes and will be able to fix them more quickly than most of your guests can, helping to avoid frustrating bottlenecks at the bar. A bartender can also take care of replenishing supplies when they run low, giving you, as host, one less thing to worry about. Finally, a savvy bartender will also make guests feel at home, adding to the hospitality of the party.

signature drinks: a classy compromise

If you want to offer more than beer and wine but are worried about the cost of a fully stocked open bar, a terrific compromise is to choose one signature mixed drink as another option for guests—such as cosmopolitans, mojitos, white Russians, or margaritas, to name a few. These can be prepared in the kitchen, and then served on passed trays or at a table. This is a great chance to be truly creative, both in the drink you choose and in the presentation.

FLOWERS

The atmosphere of every party discussed in this book can benefit from the heavenly fragrance of fresh flowers and the beauty of stylish arrangements. To figure out your flower needs, first consider the formality of the event, the season, party color schemes, if any, and your budget. (Hint: You'll always save money by staying in season, rather than having to import flowers.)

Next, think about how many arrangements you'll need. Depending on the party, this could range from one centerpiece for the dining-room table to a full array of flowers for an entire wedding reception (centerpieces, bouquets, boutonnieres, corsages, decorative flowers for the cake table, and so on).

From there, the next step is to decide whether you're going to cut and arrange the flowers yourself or use a florist.

from grocery store to green thumbs: arranging flowers yourself

I spent my childhood summers at Emily Post's former summer house on Martha's Vineyard, where her flower garden remains famous to this day. I learned a lot from my mom about how to choose flowers from the garden and arrange them in anything from a posy vase to a glass Coke bottle to a china bowl to achieve different effects. To this day, creating the flower arrangements is one of my favorite things to do when getting ready for a party. Here are a few of my tips for doing the flowers on your own:

✳ Always trim the bottoms of the stems, being sure to cut them at an angle.

✳ Start with a clean vase—no fingerprints or, worse, green gunk! Try using denture-cleaning tablets to remove residue inside glass vases (follow the directions on the box).

✳ Always use odd numbers of any particular type of flower—three roses, one tulip, for example. The total number can be even, but within varieties, keep the number odd. (I don't know what the psychology is behind this, but it is one of my mom's golden rules of flower arranging, and it works.)

✳ Keep proportion in mind. Match the size of the flowers to the vase, and the size of the arrangement to the place it's going. (Hint: Centerpieces for the table should be low enough so that guests can talk to each other over them.)

✳ Think about the structure of the arrangement. Taller, sturdier flowers can go in the center or stand alone for effect. Looser flowers should be grouped more closely so that they help support each other.

✳ Don't forget to consider using greens to fill in and help support the arrangement.

✳ Three classic arrangements are

  ✳ Bunching lots of the same flowers tightly together for a simple and classic effect (this works well with carnations, roses, and tulips, to name a few).

  ✳ Mixing colors, textures, and sizes for a more dynamic effect. This can take a more practiced eye but is worth the effort.

  ✳ A few exotic blooms alone in a vase, like calla lilies or orchids, can be very dramatic.

✳ Still stuck? Look at magazines for ideas, and then copy them as best you can. If you buy your flowers from a florist, he or she can help you identify what's in the picture when you make your purchase.

working with a florist

As fun as do-it-yourself floral arrangements might be, hiring a professional florist for your party has its advantages: Florists may have access to flowers (and prices) that you don't. They also have a professionally artistic eye and the experience to know just what works and what doesn't. If you do go this route:

- ✳ Pick someone you can trust. This bond will free the florist to be creative and do their best work.

- ✳ Bring visuals to illustrate your ideas. Showing the florist what you like (or don't like) can be very helpful in determining what's right for you.

- ✳ Have some flexibility. The flowers you had in mind may not be in season—or within your budget. Keeping an open mind will help you find something else you love if your first choice isn't available.

- ✳ Depending on the kind of event, ask if the florist will need to see the venue in advance.

- ✳ Provide any information about color, such as china or dresses, that the flowers need to be matched to.

In Lieu of Flowers

Flowers may be stunning, but they aren't your only option when it comes to party decorations. Here are a few alternatives to consider:

Silk flowers (they're beautiful *and* reusable) ✳ Pine cones ✳ Topiaries or bonsai trees ✳ Origami ✳ Glass bowls containing small koi fish or goldfish (just be sure they'll have a good home after the party!) ✳ Branches of cherry or apple blossoms ✳ Colorful fall leaves gathered in posy vases ✳ Groups of candles (try placing them on top of colorful tiles or a mirror) ✳ A basket of colorful, seasonal fruit

MUSIC

Obviously, the reception is one party where music and dancing usually play a huge role—more on that in a minute. As for the other parties, it really depends on the size and nature of the party and just how fancy you want to get.

- An *engagement party* generally requires no accompaniment, though putting some romantically oriented jazz, rock, or show music on the stereo at a low volume always makes for a nice atmosphere. For an extra-special touch, consider hiring a classical string trio or quartet.

- *Showers* are usually all about the buzz of guests and gifts—but again, some well-chosen music can add to the ambience.

- *Rehearsal dinners* tend to be music-free. On the other hand, I had a fabulous time at a rehearsal dinner where a small band had us dancing long after dessert.

- *(Bachelor)ette parties* are sure to come with their own soundtrack—probably favorites from your wilder days, played on a stereo, or whatever music is being played at the restaurant or bar where you all get together.

- At the *wedding reception*, assuming you decide to have musical entertainment (not a must, but rare is the wedding without any), the big question is whether to go with live musicians or a DJ. Each has something going for it:

  - A live band provides an immediacy and energy that can literally set the tone for the entire event. The possibilities range from rock and roll to a swing band and beyond.

  - With a DJ, what you get is maximum flexibility: Virtually any request for a popular song can be fulfilled instantly. A DJ also tends to cost only half as much as a typical band.

PHOTOGRAPHY/VIDEOGRAPHY

Everyone wants pictures to remember these various wedding parties by—but aside from the reception, hiring a professional photographer is usually out of the question, both in terms of cost and formality. How to make sure your event gets immortalized? Before the party, ask a friend or relative who enjoys taking pictures to bring along a camera—digital or otherwise—and shoot away. Another popular solution: Hand out inexpensive disposable cameras to all the guests and encourage them to go for it. Just be sure to have a convenient, well-marked spot where guests can leave the cameras when they're done. If you have a friend who's a video buff, you can encourage him or her to take some footage as well. (Note: If the event in question is a (bachelor)ette party, it may be wise to give your guests veto power over the final product.)

ask anna: how can I avoid overly posed photos?

Q: *I'm not a fan of the very posed pictures most wedding photographers produce, but I'd still like a professional to be in charge. Any suggestions?*

anna: An old roommate of mine who wanted more candid—but professional—photos of her wedding and reception chose to use a journalistic photographer. He had done weddings before, so she had an idea of what to expect, and the results were such a success that two other friends of hers have used him since. Be sure to find one with wedding experience and check out their portfolio and references first. Then don't forget to smile—you never know when they might catch *you*!

SHARING THE LOVE

And when the last guest is gone and the party is over, consider donating any flowers to local nursing homes, hospitals, or places of worship. Left-over food? Try contacting a local soup kitchen or similar charity; many are more than happy to accept donations of food. Call beforehand to check on drop-off times, so that you don't show up to a CLOSED sign. Your generosity will be appreciated!

reading the fine print
invitations

All the parties in this book start the same way: with an **invitation**. While there are **guidelines for wording**, the look and design of these invitations are up to the couple. Most couples choose to use invitations—which are, after all, a guest's introduction to their marriage—as a stylistic signature, **establishing the tone and level** of formality for the wedding to come.

APPLES AND ORANGES:
Take Your Pick

Okay, I'll admit it—I've saved every single wedding-related invitation I've ever received. The whole collection is tied together with a piece of pretty ribbon and sits on my bookcase—including invitations for showers and engagement parties. There's a cute invitation to an "around the clock" shower, with the hours of a clock face marked along the edge, and a save-the-date card with the couple's names, their wedding date, the place, and a few other words such as love arranged as a crossword puzzle, with a note on the flip side that begins: "Solving one of life's greatest puzzles..." Some of the invitations have very basic wording—such as a simple "hope you can join us" for an engagement party—while others are very formal, with tissue-paper inserts and engraved writing that asked for the "honour of my presence." One classic invitation invited me to a wedding and reception in English on the front, then again in French on the inside, since the groom and his family are from France.

Most of these invitations are printed, although there's one handwritten invitation for a farewell brunch, as well as a wedding and reception invitation with some of the most beautiful calligraphy I've ever seen. They're all "correct" and express each couple's individual style (like the wedding program bound with thin cords of climbing rope for my mountaineering friend's wedding ceremony). I guess that's why I could never pick a favorite—it would be like comparing apples to oranges.

IN A NUTSHELL:
Who's Invited to What?

This is not as complicated as it might first appear. To start with, a general piece of advice: The bride and groom should consider who their wedding guests will be *in advance of any parties*. The wedding guest list doesn't need to be finalized, but the couple should have a firm idea of who they're certain to be inviting, for a simple reason: **Anyone invited to any wedding party (office showers excepted) must be invited to the wedding.**

Apart from the reception, it's normal for most wedding parties to be smaller than the full wedding guest list, since wedding parties are typically meant to be intimate get-togethers for focused groups of friends and family. Depending on the party, the invitees might be the couple's nearest and dearest, the bride's girlfriends, or just her attendants. Whatever you do, though, *don't* invite someone to one of these parties if they're not invited to the wedding! Asking someone to any of the lead-up celebrations for a wedding but not to the wedding itself is simply rude, not to mention misleading in the extreme. Below are some party-specific guidelines:

* *Engagement parties:* Close friends and family, since guests invited to the engagement party must be invited to the wedding. That might seem like a lot to figure out so far ahead of time, but a little thought now can save you a lot of trouble later. People invited to an engagement party will naturally assume they're going to be invited to the wedding, and the last thing you want to do is raise any false expectations. For this reason, it's often best to limit the engagement party guest list, inviting only those you're sure will be invited to the wedding.

* *Showers:* Close female friends and relatives of the bride, or, if it's a Jack and Jill shower, close friends and family of the bride *and* groom.

* *(Bachelor)ette parties:* Again, close female friends and family of the bride—usually those closer to her in age, though moms and aunts have been known to make appearances. If the gathering is coed, close friends and family of both the bride and groom are invited.

* *General wedding-week parties:* Anyone in town, of the bride and groom's choosing.

* *Bridesmaids' party and groom's dinner:* The bride, her bridesmaids, and sometimes her mother; the groom, his groomsmen, and sometimes his dad.

* *Rehearsal dinner:* The parents, siblings, and any children of the bride and groom; their attendants; and the officiant. More guests, including other relatives, close friends, and (sometimes) out-of-town wedding guests, can be invited at the couple's (and their budget's) discretion.

* *Wedding reception:* Everyone!

* *Farewell brunch:* Usually everyone who was invited to the wedding; if, however, you decide to go with a select group instead, be discreet when extending invitations.

* *Belated or second reception:* Anyone who missed the wedding and/or any previous receptions.

TIMING IS EVERYTHING:
Ordering and Mailing Invitations

As a general rule, plan on at least three months for printing and delivery of formal wedding invitations, enclosures, and envelopes. (Remember, that's three months before you want to *send* the invitations—not three months before the event!) While this lead time may be reduced if you print your invitations yourself, you'll still need to give yourself time to choose (and if necessary, order) matching paper and envelopes, and to design your own layout.

When to send out wedding party invitations can vary, since it depends on the circumstances. For most wedding parties, a lead time of anywhere from three to six weeks is the average, depending on whether people will need to travel. Wedding reception invitations (most often sent with the wedding invitation itself) are usually sent six to eight weeks in advance, while invitations for a belated reception may be mailed four to eight weeks in advance—again, depending on how far guests are traveling.

The goal is to send invitations early enough so that people will be able to arrange their schedules and make travel plans, but not so early that there's no momentum built toward the event.

how to deliver the message

What type of invitation is best? For the wedding itself, it has to be a paper invitation—either printed or handwritten. For the other wedding parties, it's up to you, and depends mostly on how formal or casual a party you're planning: You wouldn't send e-mail invitations for a black-tie rehearsal dinner, nor would you be likely to send formal invitations for a backyard-barbecue engagement party.

If the party is very intimate or informal or is being put together on short notice, then a phoned or e-mailed invitation is fine, and may even be preferable. Tip: If a good number of out-of-town guests are being invited, the written invitation is still the best choice, since it's a tangible reminder of the party.

DIGITAL AGE DO'S AND DON'TS

Using e-mail or online services like Evite—which let you customize your own e-mailed invites—to send invitations for wedding parties (but not the wedding itself!) is becoming more and more common, and in the right instances, I'm all for it. There's no exact test for when it's right, but be considerate of your audience when making your choice. Inviting all of your close friends for an engagement party? Sure! Inviting your childhood friends and their mothers for a shower? You wouldn't catch me doing it.

A few other digital do's and don'ts you should be aware of:

Do...

* Try to give about two weeks' notice
* BCC everyone on your e-mailing list—it's your safest bet, what with privacy issues and people who are careless with the "Reply All" button
* Reread the message (and use spell-check!) before you hit "Send"
* Be sure to include all the information listed in "Invitation Basics" (see page 99)
* Follow up with a reminder a day or two before the event
* If using a service like Evite, fill in all the details the site asks for and remember to include a personal message
* **Make sure the e-mail addresses you use are correct, and that all your invited guests check their e-mail regularly**
* Be prepared to follow up by phone if you don't receive a prompt response—your message might have been caught in a spam filter or the recipient may not have opened it. (One of the advantages of Evite, compared with your own e-mail, is that it lets you know if the recipient has viewed the invitation yet. Very handy.)

Don't...

* Use e-mail or Evite for actual wedding invitations
* Send e-invitations to people who are Internet-challenged

gathering information

Make sure you have current mailing addresses for all of your guests before sending out invitations—otherwise, the potential confusion of undelivered invitations could lead to hurt feelings. If you don't have someone's address or need to double-check it, just ask them. It's fine to tell them why you're inquiring, if they ask—you won't spoil their enjoyment at receiving the invitation.

placing your order

Some things to remember when ordering invitations:

- Make sure your supplier can deliver invitation envelopes as soon as possible, so you can get a head start on addressing them.

- If you're working with a stationer, bring samples of the type of invitation you'd like—or at least come prepared with an idea of the level of formality you want.

- If using a stationer, be sure you have a signed contract or order form that details exactly what services will be provided and when the proofs and final product will be delivered. (See "Signing on the Dotted Line: Contracts," page 81.)

- Mistakes happen, so order at least a dozen extra invitations and envelopes (if you are handwriting your invitations) or just the envelopes (if the invitations are printed). You may want to order additional extras to have as keepsakes as well.

- Remember that RSVPs and/or gifts will be sent to the reply address you provide, so be sure that the people at that address—you, your parents, etc.—are prepared to accept and keep track of them.

- When addressing wedding invitations, you'll need the full names and titles for all guests; be sure all spellings are correct, and begin checking this information early, so you'll have time to make confirmations if need be.

invitation basics

Unlike wedding invitations, which have lots of specific wording requirements, invitations for most wedding parties are really just like any other party invitation. Here are some tips on what to include:

- ✳ What kind of party it is (cocktails, brunch, etc.)
- ✳ Why you're throwing it (a shower, a bachelorette party, etc.)
- ✳ Who the party is honoring (especially important if you think the invitee might not know the host)
- ✳ When it's being held (including day and time)
- ✳ The location (including the street address and directions, if necessary)
- ✳ Information about attire, if needed (black tie, casual, etc.)
- ✳ It's okay to ask for a reply by a certain date

- If you'd like replies phoned or e-mailed (instead of sent by regular mail), be sure to provide the appropriate phone number or e-mail address

- Use common sense if mentioning gifts. Shower invitations can mention the theme and even a corresponding "assignment," such as a room of the house or a letter of the alphabet. Registry information, however, should be included on a separate piece of paper. It's never okay to list specific gift suggestions. And while it's all right to note "No gifts, please" on invitations for events such as an engagement party, **wedding invitations should always remain free of any kind of reference to gifts—even a "No gifts, please" request.**

SEAL OF APPROVAL

Using sealing wax on the closed flap of the envelope is an easy way to lend invitations a sense of formality and polish. With hundreds of designs and colored waxes to choose from, the options abound. The only downside is that the seals can sometimes break in the mail. If you're concerned about this, consider using an ink stamp instead: You'll have all the same designs and colors to choose from, without the worry.

FRAME OF REFERENCE:
Sample Invitations

When it comes to invitations for non-reception parties, there are no fixed rules regarding style or punctuation. Here are some possible examples of various types of invitations for pre- and post-wedding parties, all of which are correct (reception invitations are covered on page 105):

PRINTED INVITATION

Please join us for cocktails to
celebrate the engagement
of our daughter
Jessica Caroline Summers
to
Ryan Adams
Saturday, August 4th
7 PM
Jack and Stephanie Summers
42 Hillyer Street
Portland, Oregon

RSVP 516-555-8367

— OR —

SUSAN AND AL COLE INVITE YOU
TO JOIN THEM FOR
SARA AND DAVID'S REHEARSAL DINNER
FRIDAY, OCTOBER 14TH
AT THE CHARLOTTE BOATHOUSE
21 BAYVIEW ROAD, CHARLOTTE

RSVP 802-555-3895

— OR —

Please join us
for a farewell brunch
on Sunday, June 6th
10 AM to 1 PM
Sally and Jeff Jacobs
41 State Street
San Francisco

RSVP 415-555-2274

FILL-IN INVITATION

for: *A shower for Elizabeth!*

date: *Saturday, May 16*

time: *4 p.m.*

place: *Caroline's house, 55 Walker Way,*
Essex Falls

RSVP: *to Caroline Humphries at*
802-555-9481 by May 5

HANDWRITTEN INVITATION

Dear Joe,

Please join us for dinner at our home on Thursday, May 7, at 8 o'clock to celebrate our daughter Jocelyn's engagement to Drew Connolly! RSVP to 202-555-4332.

Cheers,

Nancy

PHONED INVITATION

"Hi, Mrs. Nevins—this is Kate Johnson. You may have already heard, but I wanted to share the news with you myself that Josh and I are engaged! To celebrate, Mom and Dad are throwing us a cocktail party on September 14, and we hope that you and Mr. Nevins can join us. The party will be at the Waverly Inn, located at 76 Willard Street, starting at eight o'clock. Please let me know by September third if you'll be able to join us—I hope you can! My number is 516-555-7834. Bye!"

E-MAILED INVITATION

From: Audrey Summers

To: (BCC everyone!)

Subject: **You're invited to a bachelorette party for Jessica!**

Date: Saturday, January 27, 2007

Hi, everyone!

Jessica's wedding is just around the corner, and you're invited to help her have one last night out with the girls as a single lady on Saturday, February 17. The plan is to start by treating her to dinner at the Main Street Bistro at 8 PM, and then we'll go for drinks afterward. Please let me know if you can attend by February 11 so that I can make a reservation. Hope you can make it!

Audrey

RECEPTION AND
BELATED RECEPTION INVITATIONS

Invitations for wedding receptions held on the same day as the wedding (and where all the wedding guests are invited to the reception as well) are usually placed directly on the wedding invitation itself, as in this example of a formal invitation:

Mr. and Mrs. David Wilson
request the honour of your presence
at the marriage of their daughter
Eliza Jane
to
Mr. Stephen Dempsey
Saturday, the ninth of April
two thousand and eight
at five o'clock
St. Mary's Cathedral
Dorset
and afterward at the reception
Dorset Country Club

RSVP

They may also be issued on a simple card enclosed with the wedding invitation. This is sometimes done when the ceremony and the reception are held at different locations (though it's not required; the above example is also for a reception at a different location) or when the guest list for the ceremony is larger than that for the reception, in which case the reception cards are added only to the wedding invitations of those guests who are also invited to the reception. The most commonly used form is:

RECEPTION

IMMEDIATELY FOLLOWING THE CEREMONY

KNOLLS COUNTRY CLUB

LAKE FOREST

THE FAVOUR OF A REPLY IS REQUESTED

An invitation for a belated reception is sent separately and might look like this:

Mr. and Mrs. David Mathis

request the pleasure of your company

at a reception

in honor of

Mr. and Mrs. George Hill

Saturday, the twenty-fourth of July

two thousand and eight

at seven o'clock

Lake Champlain Yacht Club

Shelburne

RSVP

FORMAL FACTS

Though it may feel as though life in general keeps getting more and more casual, formal invitations are still used for many occasions—and not just for wedding invitations, either. If you choose to send formal invitations:

✳ Use high-quality card stock in cream or white (though pastels are also acceptable nowadays). Colored borders are okay, but never use black—this is reserved for death announcements.

✳ The most distinguishing feature of a formal invitation is that it is issued in the third person. (See "Ask Anna: Formal Replies," page 108.)

✳ All numbers, dates, and times are spelled out in full, except for street numbers greater than nine, which are written numerically. Listing the year is optional on all formal invitations (including for weddings), unless the event date falls in a different year from when the invitation is being sent (for example, mailing in December for January).

✳ *Honour* and *favour* really are spelled the British way, with a *u*. (Note: *honour* is only used for events held at places of worship: "the honour of your presence…")

✳ It's okay to include a request for a reply.

ask anna: formal replies

Q: *Help! I received a very formal invitation to a wedding and reception, and my mom says I need to write a formal reply. How do I do this?*

anna: A formal invitation to a party or wedding—easy to spot because it's worded in the third person ("Mr. and Mrs. Craig Jamison request the pleasure of your company...")—does indeed require a more formal reply. Using stationery (personalized or store-bought), send back a short note, also written in the third person, with all words—including days and times—spelled out in full.

The following formula is quite standard, and there's almost no need to deviate from it:

Ms. Libby Burke

accepts with pleasure [or *regrets she is unable to accept*]

Mr. and Mrs. Craig Jamison's

kind invitation

for Saturday, the twenty-third of September

at half after four o'clock [don't include this line when sending a regret]

— OR —

Ms. Libby Burke

accepts with pleasure [or *regrets she is unable to accept*]

the kind invitation of

Mr. and Mrs. Craig Jamison

for Saturday, the twenty-third of September

at half after four o'clock [don't include this line when sending a regret] ❦

In Your Honor. If someone else is hosting a wedding party for you, you'll be asked for names and addresses of people to invite. Check with your host to get an idea of what size party they're thinking of, and respect their limits. Then sit back and relax—because unless you're specifically asked to help, your host will take care of the planning from there!

Ahead of the Game: Save the date. Save-the-date cards are brief notes (usually printed) sent to people so they can hold open the day of an event that's still a long way off. Since the actual invitations won't be sent until a time closer to the actual date, this ensures that they won't make any other plans for the big day. Save-the-date cards are completely optional and are basically a safety measure in a world were people often make plans far in advance. The one iron-clad rule is that if a save-the-date card has been sent to someone, an invitation must follow at some point—you can't change your mind about inviting them later.

One terrific new trend (again, completely optional!) is to hand out creative save-the-date reminders for the wedding at the end of the engagement party. If the wedding date has been set, it's a fun way of alerting people to mark their calendars. Here are a few ideas to get you started:

- A card with a photo of the couple and save-the-date info
- Save-the-date refrigerator magnets
- Matchboxes with save-the-date info (if you like, you can also have "A perfect match!" printed on the cover)
- Little boxed cakes or chocolates with "A taste of what's to come" printed on the box, along with save-the-date info

Put Your Stamp on It. Literally! There are services, usually found online, that will produce personalized stamps for weddings and other occasions. You might use a photo of the couple, for example, or maybe a monogram of their initials intertwined. You pay the cost of the postage, plus a fee for the service. Frivolous, yes—but fun!

all about party gifts
and those all-important thank-yous

With so many contingencies regarding **what gifts** should be given at **which** of the different **wedding parties**, it's all too easy to forget why we give these gifts in the first place. A wedding-related gift isn't about worrying that you've picked the right thing or about competing with other gift-givers—it's about making a thoughtful gesture to people you love.

IN A NUTSHELL:
When Should You Give a Gift?

* *Engagement parties:* As a general rule, gifts are not given at an engagement party. (Close friends and relatives of the bride and groom may want to give them an engagement gift, in which case it should be presented to the couple in private.) **This tradition is currently in a state of change**, however. Depending on where you live, giving a gift at the engagement party may now be expected. Check with your host if you're unsure what to do.

* *Showers:* You absolutely should bring a gift to a wedding shower. (That's the whole point of the party, after all!) If there's a gift theme, try to stick to it—it will be more fun for the bride and the other guests that way. If you can't attend the shower, you don't need to send a gift, but you can if you'd like.

- *(Bachelor)ette parties:* Gifts aren't necessary at (bachelor)ette parties, although the hosts may choose to provide guests with some inexpensive token gift to remember the evening by.

- *Attendants' parties:* Although no gifts are expected at these parties, they can be an opportunity for the bride and groom to exchange gifts with their attendants; this may also be done at the rehearsal dinner (see next item).

- *Rehearsal dinners:* Guests do not bring gifts for the rehearsal dinner. However, the bride and groom may exchange gifts with their attendants at this time.

- *Wedding receptions:* Gifts are always given by invited guests to the bride and groom on the occasion of their wedding, even if a guest can't attend. Gifts may be sent before the date to whatever address the bride and groom designate or may be brought to the wedding and left wrapped with an accompanying card on the gifts table. A wedding gift can also be sent after the fact, but this should be done as soon as possible. (See "Ask Anna: Do I Have One Year to Send a Wedding Gift?" page 113.)

- *Farewell brunches:* Gifts are not given at brunch the day after the wedding. In addition, wedding gifts that have already been opened should *not* be displayed at the brunch.

- *Belated receptions:* There's an important distinction to be made here: Gifts are given because of *weddings*, not because of *receptions*. If a guest is invited only to a belated reception and not to the wedding itself, then a gift doesn't officially need to be given (though if the reception is honoring a close family member or friend, you'll probably want to give one anyway). If, on the other hand, you were also invited to the wedding and haven't yet given the couple a wedding present, then, yes, a gift at a belated reception is appropriate. If you were invited to the wedding and have already sent a wedding present (or brought one to a previous reception), you don't need to bring a second gift to the belated reception. In short, think about it this way: **One *wedding* invitation, one present**.

* *Destination weddings:* Wedding presents are given if you've been invited to a destination wedding. However, since attending one can be very expensive, it's okay to spend a bit less on the gift than you'd normally consider. In fact, because of this expense, many couples will ask those guests who made the trip not to give them presents at all.

ask anna: do I have one year to send a wedding gift?

Q: *I haven't had time to find a gift for my friends prior to their wedding. But I have up to a year after their wedding to send a gift—right?*

anna: No, not really. As I mentioned earlier (see "Wedding Gifts," page 49), the idea that you have a year in which to send a wedding gift is a myth. Ideally, you should either send your gift before the wedding or bring it to the reception. If you haven't given a gift by the time the wedding is held, send one as soon as you can. And while I'm not endorsing the one-year rule, the bottom line is: Better late than never. I've heard from a lot of couples who were really hurt that one of their guests didn't send a present. This isn't about greed for gifts; the fact is, lack of a gift translates into a feeling that the guest must not care enough to bother. In the end, it's *always* best to send a gift—no matter *how* late it is—along with a note apologizing for the delay.

HOW MUCH SHOULD YOU SPEND ON GIFTS?

How much you choose to spend on a present—*any* present—is always up to you. There's no etiquette rule or formula for figuring out how much you should spend on a gift for a shower or wedding. Instead, *think about your budget and your relationship with the person.* Don't feel guilty if you want to spend more on your sister than on your second cousin. How you choose to budget for presents to the bride and groom is your own private business and no one else's.

REGISTRIES AND THEIR PUBLIC PRICE TAGS

When I give the advice in the preceding section, I sometimes hear: "But if I buy something from their registry, won't they know how much I spent anyway?" Technically, this is true—but you still shouldn't worry. Most of us have been trained from childhood to remove the price tag from a gift before we give it, and this is a good rule of thumb—after all, the gesture of giving is what counts, not the dollar amount of the gift. With registries, where the price of the gift is known to all (including the bride and groom), having your financial choices made public may leave you concerned that you'll be judged on how much you spent. Relax: You won't be. Remember, the bride and groom are going to be so busy getting ready for their wedding that it's unlikely they'll remember the amount of each gift. Besides, by making your purchase from a registry, you're guaranteed that the couple is going to like whatever you pick!

Keep in mind, too, that if you still prefer not to choose something from the registry, it's perfectly fine to go with something else instead. Registries are just a guide, not a required shopping list. A gift is always a thoughtful and welcome gesture, no matter what you decide to give.

registries: spreading the word

Now that the bride—or groom—has taken the time to drag their intended through three different stores and has thoroughly debated which bathroom towels will best express their personalities, how do they let their guests know where they're registered? Since gifts should *never* be mentioned in a wedding invitation, word of mouth is the way to go.

Brides (and grooms): Make a point of letting your family, close friends, and attendants know where you're registered (or if you're *not* registered anywhere), so they can tell guests when asked.

Parents, family, close friends, and attendants of the couple: Ask them where they're registered, if they haven't already told you, then spread the word as far and wide as you can.

For shower registries, it gets a little easier: As mentioned in "Ask Anna: Can I List Registry Info on the Shower Invitation?" (page 22), it's okay to include information about gift registries along with the shower invitation—just don't print the information on the invitation itself.

As a guest, it's absolutely okay to ask the couple, their attendants, or their close family where they're registered—and, if they aren't registered, what they might like instead. In fact, it's what you're supposed to do; since they can't put gift information on the invitations and you aren't a mind reader, how else *could* you know? All of these people should have the pertinent information on hand.

There have been a number of times when I've called couples or their friends or family, to ask where they're registered. Sometimes I've gone with a registry item and sometimes with something of my own choosing—such as those Simon Pearce vases I love to give.

WHAT GIFT TO GIVE?

If you aren't choosing a gift from a registry, then the sky is the limit as far as your options are concerned. In Part One, I offer some specific gift ideas for the different wedding parties. Remember, though, what counts is the thought, not the price tag. While wedding gifts are usually a step or two up in relation to engagement or shower gifts, which step you start on doesn't matter.

Still unsure how to proceed? Items for the home are always a safe bet—especially unique ones like a hand-crafted wood cutting board or a one-of-a-kind serving bowl or vase. That way you won't have to worry that another guest snagged the very same gift. Finally, always remember that including a gift receipt—which doesn't list the price—from the store where you bought your present is a great idea if you feel the couple may want the option of exchanging your gift for something else.

gifts of money

Giving gifts of money is becoming more common, though unless it's what the couple has asked for (and it's okay for them to ask), it's preferable for guests to choose a tangible gift, which shows not only generosity but also thoughtfulness on the part of the giver for taking the time to select a gift they think the couple might like. If a couple *does* ask for money, it's best if they let people know how they're planning to use it—on a down payment for a house, for example. Guests will feel more comfortable if they know what their check is going toward.

GIFTS IN ACTION:
At the Party

When someone gives you a gift, your natural instinct is to open it in front of them, so they can enjoy your happy reaction. Sometimes this instinct is right on: If you bring a gift to a shower, it should be opened right there at the party, oohed and ahhed over, and then passed around for all the guests to admire. Any gifts exchanged between the couple and their attendants—at whatever event they choose for the exchange—should also be opened on the spot.

When gifts are given at an engagement party or reception, however, it's best simply to thank the giver and put their present on a gift table (hosts should prepare for this by having an available table waiting—see below). This keeps the focus of the event on mingling with guests rather than on the gifts. That said, do receive each and every gift graciously, being sure to thank the giver.

GIFT TABLES

At engagement parties and receptions, gifts should be left unopened on a designated table, which is often dressed up for the occasion with a tablecloth and flowers. It's okay to just leave the gift there without actually presenting it to the couple—**just be sure to attach a card securely to your gift**. And for all of you out there with "doctor handwriting," *make sure your signature is legible*, so the couple knows who to thank!

The best way to display any gifts of money is to list the givers—but not the amounts—in a gift-record book on the gift table. Checks may be displayed (usually under glass), but the bank information and amount *must* be covered with a piece of paper. Gifts should not be displayed at belated or second receptions.

ask anna: no, really—*no gifts*

Q: *I'm asking guests not to bring gifts to my engagement party, but I'm worried that some people will anyway! What should I do if this happens?*

anna: The phrase "No gifts, please" really does mean *no gifts*. If some guests ignore this request, however, and show up with a gift in hand, you should simply smile, thank them graciously (throwing in a "You didn't have to do that!" is also certainly in order), put the gift aside to be opened later, and then just let it go. *Don't* express annoyance or refuse the gift. *Do* reassure (in private) any other guests who might be worried about not having brought a gift that they were perfectly in the right not to have done so.

THE GREAT EXCHANGE:
Other Kinds of Gifts

Not all wedding-related gifts are given by the wedding guests to the couple: Gifts given by the bride and groom to their attendants are very popular—the bride choosing gifts for her bridesmaids, the groom for his groomsmen. The bridesmaids and groomsmen may return the favor by chipping in on gifts for the bride and groom, respectively. The bride and groom may also give gifts to their parents and/or siblings and other close relatives, as tokens of their thanks and appreciation. While it's rare that gifts aren't given by the couple to their attendants, none of these gift exchanges are required—they're simply thoughtful add-ons. If, however, either the bride or groom has children from a previous marriage, I strongly recommend that they consider giving presents to them, both to include them in the wedding process and to honor the important position they hold in the new family that's being created.

the bride's and groom's gifts to their attendants

While the bride's and groom's gifts to their attendants don't have to be grandiose, a sincere token of the couple's appreciation is always welcome. And remember, these gifts are for people who have given up much of their time, planned fabulous parties, purchased formalwear and gifts, and often traveled long distances to be with the couple on their big day.

The bride usually chooses one gift that she gives to each of her bridesmaids, while the groom picks one gift that he gives to each of his groomsmen—though sometimes the couple might decide to give everyone the same thing. Many of the suggestions on the next page can be found at a variety of prices; the aim here is to give your attendants a meaningful commemoration of the occasion. (I was once lucky enough to receive a double strand of pearls for being a bridesmaid. The bride had purchased river pearls, which are much less expensive than cultured pearls but still lovely.) Gifts that are engraved are usually inscribed with the recipient's initials and/or the date of the wedding. Remember, the idea is for the engraving to be meaningful but discreet.

for the ladies	for the gents
pearl necklace or earrings	CUFFLINKS
pashmina shawl	CASHMERE SCARF
handbags to match bridesmaids' dresses	MATCHING TIES AND CUMMERBUNDS FOR THE CEREMONY
silver bracelets	ENGRAVED SILVER SWISS ARMY KNIFE
engraved silver key chains	
leather-bound photo albums	
engraved flasks	
watches	

And what about those darling flower girls and ring bearers? It's nice to have a gift (something age-appropriate—no flasks!) for them as well, to help make them feel special and part of the fun.

It's best to give these "extra" gifts before the wedding, especially if they're items being used for the ceremony (matching ties for the groomsmen or pearl earrings for the bridesmaids, for example). The reception is not a good time—things can get a little crazy, and there's even a chance they might be lost. Some couples pick a private moment sometime in the days prior to the wedding, or even that morning; others choose to present their gifts a little more publicly at one of the wedding-week parties, such as an attendants' party or the rehearsal dinner.

THANK-YOU NOTES

As a kid, I always tried to get out of writing thank-you notes—not because I didn't appreciate the present but because the writing felt too much like homework. Now, I actually enjoy the act of using pretty stationery and a good pen to jot a little note of thanks. I always appreciate receiving them, so it feels good to trust that the ones I send are also appreciated by their recipients. In a world of e-mail and online registries, a handwritten note is more than just a perfunctory courtesy; the time you take to pause for a moment and put down your thanks on paper demonstrates your appreciation just as much as the words you choose to write.

thank-you basics

While we've all had experience (I hope!) sending thank-you notes, thank-yous for wedding-related presents can introduce an all-new set of questions for the newlyweds (or soon-to-be-weds). First, what are you thanking *for*? Well, for any wedding or wedding party gifts (including gifts of money), obviously, but not just the kind that come wrapped in ribbons and bows. Thank-you notes should also be sent anytime someone throws you a party, lets you use their home to host a party or to house a wedding guest, or gives of their own time and talents to help you. For example, I've heard about many weddings where friends and families help with everything from baking the cake to taking photographs or arranging the flowers. Any of these generous acts most definitely warrants a thank-you. You should also write thank-you notes to your attendants, usually attached to any gift you might give them. And finally, don't forget your suppliers, vendors, and any other professionals you may have hired. You don't have to thank each and every one in writing, but anyone who exceeded expectations will appreciate the recognition.

The bride and groom aren't the only two people who might send wedding-related thank-yous, either. If the bridesmaids aren't local and used someone's home to host a wedding shower, for example, they should send that person a thank-you note.

thanking for two

When thanking someone for a wedding gift, remember that you're no longer thanking just for yourself but rather for two people, since the gift was given to you as a couple. It doesn't matter whether the bride or the groom writes the thank-you notes—however they wish to divvy them up is fine. If either the bride or the groom happens to know one of the guests better, then that person might be the one to pen the note, but this isn't a rule. And regardless of who composes the thank-you, both people should be mentioned as appreciating the gift—"Rob and I love the quilt you sent!"

When signing the note, it's fine for the person writing the note to sign only their name, sign for themselves and their spouse (or soon-to-be-spouse), or have each person sign their own name. Any of these options is appropriate.

thank-you note statute of limitations

Contrary to popular myth, couples don't have a grace period of a year in which to send their thanks. **All thank-you notes should be written within three months of receiving the gift.** Ideally, a response should be written the day you receive the gift. If that's not possible, try to set a daily or weekly goal—this will help you keep from falling behind and will also let you compose your note while the pleasure of opening the gift is still fresh in your mind. Besides, no one wants to come back from their honeymoon to a hundred thank-you notes still waiting to be written!

If for any reason you *haven't* sent your notes within three months, you're not off the hook—no matter how late, sending a note for a gift is still a must. Send it as soon as possible, with an apology for the delay. Any potential embarrassment over sending a late note won't be nearly so bad as the embarrassment you'll feel at never having sent one at all—not to mention the hurt that this can cause the giver.

ten thank-you note do's and don'ts

- *Do* personalize your notes, making reference to the person as well as the gift.

- *Do* be enthusiastic, though you don't need to gush. Avoid saying that a gift is the most beautiful you've ever seen, unless you really mean it.

- *Don't* send form letters or cards with printed messages and just your signature.

- *Don't* use e-mail or post generic thank-you messages on your Web site in lieu of personal notes.

- *Don't* mention that you plan to return or exchange a gift or express dissatisfaction in any way.

- *Do* mention what use you'll make of money gifts. (Referring to the amount is optional.)

- *Don't* use lateness as an excuse not to write. If you're still sending notes after your first anniversary, keep writing.

- *Do* remember that a gift should be acknowledged with the same courtesy and generosity in which it was given.

- *Do* promptly acknowledge the receipt of shipped gifts (so the sender knows it arrived safely) by mailing a note right away, or by calling and following up with a written note shortly thereafter.

- *Don't* include wedding photos or use photo cards if this means delaying sending the notes while you wait for the photos.

anatomy of a thank-you note

While there's no formula for the perfect thank-you note, the notes people remember are the ones that express real feeling. Before you write anything, think about the person or people you're thanking. How would the conversation go if you were thanking them in person? Looking at their gift as you prepare to write can also help inspire you.

Here's an example of a good thank-you note, with the key elements marked:

Dear Mr. and Mrs. Putnam,

I'm looking right now [great way to focus on the gift] *at the lovely silver candlestick holders* [mentions gift in a complimentary, nongushy fashion] *you sent and picturing how nice they will look with lighted candles on our Thanksgiving table next month.* [shows how the gift will be used] *(We're hosting Sam's family for the first time!) They really are just right, and Sam and I are so grateful to you.* [official thanks from both of you]

We were both so sorry that you couldn't come to the wedding, but I know your trip to New Zealand must have been amazing! [includes a personal, conversational note] *If all goes according to plan, we will be in San Francisco for Christmas. We'd love to see you and the girls then and hear about your travels.* [plans to keep in touch]

Again, thank you so much for the lovely candlestick holders and for the beautiful words in your note. [acknowledges a thoughtful gesture]

Love from both of us, [includes the groom]

Courtney

ask anna: what's the etiquette of thanking someone twice?

Q: *Do I have to send a thank-you note if I've already thanked the giver in person?*

anna: Yes. This question comes up most often with wedding showers, though it can apply at other parties, too. The old rule was that if you thanked someone for a gift in person, you didn't have to send a thank-you note, since your thanks had already been expressed. Nowadays, however, the expectation is that a note will also be sent—so even if you've thanked the giver in person or over the phone, be sure to mail a note as well, to avoid any confusion or hurt feelings. As mentioned earlier, writing a thank-you note is a way of paying respect to the giver by taking a moment of your time to reflect on their gift and compose an individualized message of thanks.

Choosing Thank-You Note Stationery. There's no "official" stationery for thank-you notes, though you'll probably want to use a standard one-sided or single-fold note card with matching envelope. The paper should be white, ecru, ivory, or a light color, and you should use ink that's easy to read (black is always legible). Traditionally, the paper would be plain or have a colored border, but nowadays a card with a design on it is fine, as long as the design is tasteful and won't distract from the note itself. If the bride is using monogrammed stationery, any notes sent before the wedding should use her maiden initials, while notes mailed after the wedding should use her married initials (if the bride is changing her name).

it takes two

the perfect host,
the perfect guest

Being a **good host** or a **good guest** really gets to the heart of what etiquette is all about. This kind of knowledge goes beyond knowing what fork to use (which Emily didn't really care about, and neither do I) to thinking about how you interact with the people around you. After all, this is why we get together in the first place: to enjoy one another's company.

Whether you're a host or a guest at any of the wedding parties outlined in this book, being aware of a few **basic guide-lines**, such as **sending in your RSVP** in a timely fashion and **knowing how to make introductions**, will help keep everything moving smoothly—allowing you to spend your time focusing on the people you're with rather than worrying about what to do or say.

THE PERFECT HOST

The invitations have been sent, the flowers arranged, and the hors d'oeuvres prepared. Now that guests are coming up the walk, it's your job to direct the party, by greeting people as they arrive, making introductions, moving conversations along, and making sure that any food and drinks are being served properly. The very best hosts make it all seem effortless. Whether this is your first time hosting or your fiftieth, here are some guidelines to see you through all the basic situations.

hosting 101

- Be ready at the hour indicated on the invitation—don't count on late arrivals. Take care of cleaning up and getting dressed ahead of time. If you're not hosting in your own home, be at the venue before the start time, in case anyone shows up early.

- Wait at or near the entrance to greet and welcome your guests when they arrive.

- Be prepared—drinks and food should always be ready to go before the first guest arrives. You don't want to miss your own party because you're running around taking care of last-minute details.

- Circulate among your guests, taking time to chat with everyone.

- Make it a point to introduce guests who don't know each other, staying for a moment to help get the conversation going.

- Keep an eye on the clock when it comes to serving food, and on guests' glasses, offering to refill drinks.

- Let the event have some room to flow. Schedules are important, but don't be ridiculous about it. The best hosts allow a party to move at its own pace, rather than holding it to a rigid timetable.

- Don't forget to anticipate the little things, like stocking the bathroom with fresh towels, extra toilet paper, and a fresh bar of soap.

ask anna: what do I do if a guest wants to bring kids?

Q: *When my fiancé and I get married next month, the only children we're planning to invite are our nieces and nephews. We just heard from some close friends, who asked if they could bring their kids to the wedding. I really don't want them to, but I'm not sure how to turn them down. What should I say?*

anna: Simple: Just tell them sorry, but the wedding is an adults-only affair except for your immediate family. If they're traveling from out of town as a family, you can also offer to help locate a babysitter to watch their kids during the wedding. Once you've indicated that children aren't invited to a wedding or any other event, it's best not to make any exceptions. If you do, the other guests—who didn't ask and just found sitters—will be annoyed that you let someone else bring their kids. As it is, by asking you to overlook the "no children" rule in their case, your friends are putting you in an awkward position.

making introductions

Parties for weddings often bring together people from the couple's lives who might not meet otherwise, so it's important to introduce guests who haven't met each other before, especially since some guests may not know *anyone* except the couple.

When making an introduction, try to think of something to say about each person beyond just their name—this can often help jump-start their conversation: "Alicia, this is my friend John, from college. John, Alicia and I used to take art classes together."

In most cases, the order in which the introduction is made doesn't matter. There used to be lots of rules about who should be introduced to whom, but the only real modern translation of this would involve introducing a younger person to a significantly older person (think in terms of generations here)—in which case you turn to the older person and address them first: "Mrs. Phillips, I'd like you to meet my friend Katherine Davies." Similarly, you would introduce other guests *to* a real VIP, such as a senator, bishop, or judge: "Senator Smith, I'd like to introduce to you my friend Matt Chambers."

MAKING A GRAND ENTRANCE

To make an impression before your guests even step through the door, line your front walk or entryway with . . .

Tiki torches

Little white Christmas lights

Chinese lanterns

Luminaria (candles set inside small paper bags that have been filled with sand)

Rose petals (just be careful not to spread them on the walkway—
they can be very slippery)

Seashells

Colorful fall leaves

priority seating

As a host, one decision you'll need to make is how to seat your guests. If you're throwing a **cocktail party with passed-tray service**, this issue is usually moot, since guests will be mingling throughout—either standing or, if they do choose to sit, finding anywhere that's handy. If you're planning a **buffet-style meal**, then you'll need to decide whether to go this same informal route (leaving guests to balance plates of food on their laps) or provide table settings where guests can sit down to eat. Finally, if you're serving a **plated meal**, then guests by definition will be seated around tables.

Once table settings enter the picture, you'll need to decide whether to let guests seat themselves wherever they choose or give everyone an assigned seat. There are pros and cons to each: The "sit where you want" approach means guests will feel freer to switch places and conversation partners as the meal progresses, while assigned seating gives you a chance to shape your guests' interactions and also removes the awkward uncertainty that can otherwise occur. (Even with assigned seating, by the way, it's fine if guests want to switch seats for dessert and coffee.)

There are no rules about which approach to use, but in general, the larger or more formal the event, the more likely it is that you'll want to give some kind of guidance. For a smaller gathering (say, a dinner party), it often makes sense to place individual guests' place cards directly on the table at their assigned seats. At larger events, one common practice is to give people assigned tables. In this case, a table number is usually written on each guest's place card, with the cards arranged on a table near the entrance to the dining area. Each guest then chooses who they'd like to sit next to at their table.

If you do go with assigned seats, there are a few guidelines to keep in mind. Guests of honor should be seated to the host's immediate right. If a couple is being honored by another couple, then the man would sit to the right of the hostess, and the woman to the right of the host. And if a couple is being honored by one person, the honoree of the opposite sex of the host sits to the host's immediate right, and the honoree of the same sex to the host's left. (Phew!) After that, seats are assigned at your choosing but typically go boy-girl-boy-girl. Try to keep a balanced mix in your seating arrangements, so that you have some of the usual suspects seated next to each other but also some unusual pairings— such as a botanist sitting next to a stockbroker.

Whether you assign seats or just tables, the bride and groom should always be placed together. If either of their sets of parents is divorced, the divorced parents should *not* be seated together (unless they're on good terms) but *should* be seated with their new spouses, live-ins, etc. In fact, it's a general rule of thumb that any spouses, fiancé(e)s, or live-ins should be seated with each other.

seating at the reception

At the wedding reception, even if you choose not to have assigned seating for the other guests, a special table is typically set aside for the wedding party itself, and often for the parents and other close relatives of the bride and groom as well.

The wedding party's table is usually set at one end of the room. If the table is rectangular, then the party sits along one side of the table facing the room, with the bride and groom seated at the center of the table (the bride on the groom's right). The maid or matron of honor sits on the groom's left, the best man on the bride's right, and the rest of the bridesmaids and ushers alternate out from there.

If the group is very large—or if the attendants' significant others are joining them at the table—then a U-shaped table (with the bride and groom seated at the bend of the U) or two round tables (with the bride and groom joined at one table by the maid of honor, the best man, and their partners) may be used instead.

If you also choose to have separate parents' tables for the bride's immediate family (parents, grandparents, and other close relatives) and for the groom's immediate family, these are typically placed near or alongside the table where the wedding party is seated.

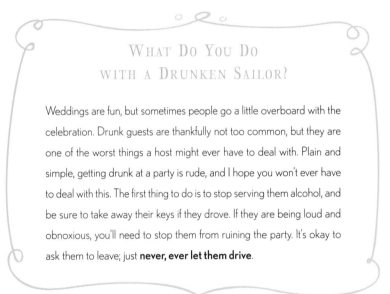

WHAT DO YOU DO WITH A DRUNKEN SAILOR?

Weddings are fun, but sometimes people go a little overboard with the celebration. Drunk guests are thankfully not too common, but they are one of the worst things a host might ever have to deal with. Plain and simple, getting drunk at a party is rude, and I hope you won't ever have to deal with this. The first thing to do is to stop serving them alcohol, and be sure to take away their keys if they drove. If they are being loud and obnoxious, you'll need to stop them from ruining the party. It's okay to ask them to leave; just **never, ever let them drive**.

THE PERFECT GUEST

There's a lot of advice swirling around on how to be a charming and efficient host, but it's easy to forget that being a good guest is just as important—and maybe even more so, since we all spend a lot more time attending parties than we do throwing them. Here are some pointers to keep in mind whenever you attend a party, wedding-related or otherwise.

how to read an invitation

A well-written invitation should give you all the information you'll need to know—such as who's throwing the party, the date and time, and where it's being held. But people still often get confused about *who* is actually invited, particularly when it comes to wedding invitations, where budgets and head counts really come into play. So here's the rule, once and for all: **In a wedding invitation, the names on the envelope are *literally* the people being invited—no one else.**

If your invitation simply says "Ms. Tara O'Connor," then you are the only person invited—period. If it says "Ms. Tara O'Connor and Guest," then it's you plus one. (The choice is up to you who that one other person is, but if you are engaged or have a live-in, the idea is usually for you to bring your significant other.) Children are invited *only* if the invite says "Mr. and Mrs. Javier Chavez *and family*," or if the kids' names are spelled out on the next lines of the envelope. Even if the party is informal, you shouldn't presume that children are invited without first checking with your host, unless it's been clearly stated.

RSVP!

RSVP is an abbreviation of the French phrase *répondez, s'il vous plaît*, which translates to "the favor of a reply is requested"—or simply, "please reply." In other words, responding to a request for an RSVP means letting your host know whether you can attend. **If your invitation asks for an RSVP, just do it— please!** One of the biggest complaints I hear for any kind of party is that all too often, those invited never respond to their hosts.

If a phone number is given after the letters *RSVP* or the words "please reply," then your host would prefer a phone call. Same goes for an e-mail or mailing address. If no phone number or address is listed on the invitation, send a short note to the return address on the envelope: "Andy and I will be happy to attend Monica and Brad's engagement party next month. Thanks for thinking of us, and see you soon!" (For replies to formal invitations, see "Ask Anna: Formal Replies," page 108.)

If you can't make the event, you don't have to give a reason unless you want to; a simple "I'm so sorry I won't be able to be there" will suffice. If your invitation was sent via e-mail, just reply back—only to the host, *not* to "reply all"!—with a short note.

No waiting until the last minute, either; your hosts need to figure out the party's head count for planning and budgeting purposes, and it's rude to keep them waiting. It's even okay to reply the very day you receive the invitation. (Don't worry about appearing overeager; your hosts will feel good knowing that people received their invitations and that you'll be able to come.) If the RSVP request is followed by a "reply by" date, do your host the favor of responding by that date. If there's no "reply by" date, send your response as soon as you know your answer—but no later than two weeks in advance.

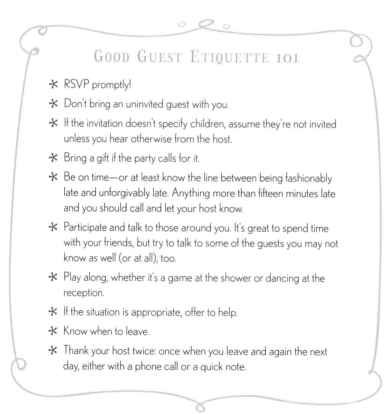

GOOD GUEST ETIQUETTE 101

✻ RSVP promptly!

✻ Don't bring an uninvited guest with you.

✻ If the invitation doesn't specify children, assume they're not invited unless you hear otherwise from the host.

✻ Bring a gift if the party calls for it.

✻ Be on time—or at least know the line between being fashionably late and unforgivably late. Anything more than fifteen minutes late and you should call and let your host know.

✻ Participate and talk to those around you. It's great to spend time with your friends, but try to talk to some of the guests you may not know as well (or at all), too.

✻ Play along, whether it's a game at the shower or dancing at the reception.

✻ If the situation is appropriate, offer to help.

✻ Know when to leave.

✻ Thank your host twice: once when you leave and again the next day, either with a phone call or a quick note.

what to wear?

We've all been there—including me. It's bad enough standing in front of your closet on an average day thinking, "What on earth am I going to wear?" But when you're going to a party and you have no idea what others will be wearing, the uncertainty can feel much worse.

The solution: First, see if your host has included instructions on the invitation, such as "casual" or "black tie." If so, do them the favor of complying (see "Party Attire: From Casual to Black Tie," below, for guidelines). If not, try gauging the formality of the invitation itself. If you're still stuck, it really is okay to call your host and ask what the dress guidelines are. No one expects you to read minds. If you're not sure what attire is appropriate, a simple question such as "Tom, how formal is your engagement party going to be?" or "Juliet, is this a skirts-and-dresses-type shower or more of a jeans-and-a-nice-sweater sort of thing?" should set you right.

PARTY ATTIRE: FROM CASUAL TO BLACK TIE

	CASUAL/INFORMAL	SEMIFORMAL	FORMAL/BLACK TIE
Gents	Nice jeans or pants with collared shirt and/or sweater; jacket optional; no tie	Dark suit; or dress slacks, sport jacket or blazer, and tie	If the invite says *black tie*, then a tuxedo is a must. If it just says *formal*, then a dark suit or tuxedo is okay.
Ladies	Nice jeans, pants, or skirt with simple top or sweater; or day dress	Dressy pants or skirt with nice top; or day or cocktail dress, depending on the time of day	Long evening dress or dressy cocktail dress. And yes, black is okay.
What not to wear	Avoid T-shirts except for the most informal parties, where you're sure it'll be okay. No ripped, stained, or wrinkled clothes.	No jeans, no floor-length gowns	A word to the wise: **Tuxedos are traditionally worn only after 6 pm***

*The only exception is for a late-afternoon wedding followed by a formal evening reception—clearly guests won't be changing their clothes, so it's okay to wear a tuxedo, since you are anticipating the reception.

Taking Matters Into Your Own Hands: How to Introduce Yourself. I'll be honest—introducing myself to strangers isn't my favorite thing to do. But at a party where you don't know anyone else, introducing yourself to other guests sure beats standing alone. It's actually quite simple: Just look for some people who seem interesting to you, then mosey on over. Unless they're completely clueless, they'll probably turn to acknowledge you. If they don't, just wait for a break in the conversation to smile and say something along the lines of "Hi, I'm Anna. I'm a friend of the bride's." Asking how they know the couple getting married is usually the best icebreaker with wedding parties.

If it's simply too intimidating for you to walk up to a stranger, try hanging out by the food or drinks and making a comment to someone else waiting in line, such as "Great food!" or "Wow, can you believe this weather?" Yes, it's pretty innocuous—but exchanging a little small talk makes it easier to then introduce yourself. If the other person doesn't pick up on your overture and just walks away, don't take it personally. The fault is theirs, not yours—so put your chin up, smile, and try again.

ask anna: should I tip at an open bar?

Q: *I'm going to a wedding reception next month, and there's going to be an open bar. Should I still bring along some cash to tip the bartenders with?*

anna: No. "Open bar" means the host is taking care of every-thing, and that includes tipping the bartender appropriately at the end of the event. Of course, it's always fine to offer a tip on top of that, if you thought the bartender took especially good care of you and you really want to express your gratitude.

cheers!

making toasts

Some people are naturals at giving toasts, while others need a little help. There are all kinds of approaches and styles, but to strike the right tone you'll need to think about what you want to say in advance. Here are some tips on **which parties call for toasts, who might give them**, and **what to say**—or *not* **to say**!

THREE PARTIES WHERE TOASTS ARE A MUST

While toasts are appropriate at any wedding party, there are three events where toasts are absolutely required: The *engagement party*, the *rehearsal dinner*, and the *wedding reception*.

toasting at the engagement party

At the engagement party, the first toast is made by the father of the bride, in the form of an announcement of the engagement. This typically occurs midway through the party, once all of the guests have arrived and have had a chance to mingle for a bit.

> *Thanks for coming, everyone. My wife Carol and I are so happy*
> *to have you all here. We'd like to take this opportunity to*
> *formally announce that our daughter, Abby, and her boyfriend,*
> *Steve, are engaged to be married!*

Since it's likely that the guests already have heard the big news, the bride's father will also typically use this moment to extend his warm wishes to the couple and the assembled guests, especially the family of the groom.

> *I want you all to join me in raising a glass to Abby and Steve*
> *and wishing them a wonderful and fulfilling life together. I also*
> *want to welcome Steve's parents and tell them how nice it's been*
> *to get to know them and how thrilled I am that our families will*
> *be united.*

If the groom's parents are there, a toast from his father is also a nice touch. If the host is someone other than the parents of the bride or groom, he or she may wish to say a few words as well. After this, the floor is open to other family members and friends to toast the couple. The couple themselves may also wish to raise a glass to their hosts, their future in-laws, and/or their guests. Finally, if the couple wants to (and has already made their selections), they can announce the members of their wedding party at this time.

toasting at the rehearsal dinner

At the rehearsal dinner, the first toast is made by the dinner's host—usually the groom's father. This toast often occurs during the main course:

> *I'd like to thank you all for joining us this evening. We're so*
> *happy to begin celebrating Kate and Martin's marriage. Here's*
> *to our wonderful new daughter-in-law, Kate, and our incredibly*
> *fortunate son, Martin! We'd also like to thank Kate's parents,*
> *Thomas and Virginia Johnson, for making us feel so welcome.*

This toast is often met by a "return toast" from the father of the bride. A whole slew of other toasts may then follow. Unlike the wedding reception—when toasts should generally be short and to the point—the rehearsal dinner is a time when longer toasts and stories are welcome. Those making toasts might include the mothers of the bride and groom, the best man and the maid/matron of honor (these toasts may coincide with presenting attendants' gifts to the bride and groom), and other wedding attendants, close friends, and relatives. If the bride and groom are giving gifts to their attendants at the rehearsal dinner, they may want to toast their attendants at this time, as well.

toasting at the reception

Traditionally, the first toast at the wedding reception is made by the best man. This is the most formal of all wedding-related toasts, and it occurs only after all the wedding guests have been provided with glasses of champagne. At a sit-down dinner, the toast takes place as soon as everyone is seated. At a cocktail reception, the best man's toast is made after the couple enters the reception. As mentioned above, the reception toast should be brief, lasting no more than a few minutes. It may include a short speech, followed by a salute to the couple:

> *To Wendy and Sam—two very special people. May you always be as happy as you are today.*

It's fine if the best man's toast is the only one made. Often, however, the fathers of the bride and groom will also toast each other's families and the marriage of their children. The maid/matron of honor may offer a toast as well, and the bride and groom may choose to toast their families and each other.

ask anna: may I have your attention, please!

Q: *How do I get everyone's attention when I'm giving a toast?*

anna: Avoid tapping on your glass with your dinner knife—while tempting, this may leave you with no glass left to toast with. A better approach is simply to stand up and ask for everyone's attention (repeatedly, if you have to), then wait patiently until the conversation dies down and all eyes are on you. (Whatever you do, just learn from Bridget Jones and don't get frustrated and shout, "*Oy!*")

RAISE YOUR GLASSES:
Three Surefire Ways to Make a Toast

Okay—now that you *do* have their attention, what do you say? No matter how tongue-tied you feel, you'll never go wrong if you keep it short and sweet. A great speech should not take more than a minute or so and can be as short as a few lines:

> *I'd like to take a moment to congratulate Julie and Mike on their*
> *engagement! Let's raise our glasses and toast to long life and*
> *much happiness and love for them both. To Julie and Mike!*

Think you're funny? Cracking jokes and telling funny stories about the bride and/or groom is fine; just keep it light and clean and approach it with good intentions—don't seek to make anyone genuinely uncomfortable:

> *I've known Mike since the third grade. When we were kids, he*
> *was famous for telling everyone, "You're not the boss of me!"*
> *Well, Mike, I hate to break it to you, but Julie really is the boss*
> *of you now! Cheers to you both!*

And of course there are the tear-jerking toasts. If you want to express strong emotions (the good kind, of course), there are few better opportunities—but if it doesn't feel natural, don't force yourself. It's okay if you get a little choked up yourself; composure is great, but so is honest, heartfelt emotion. The biggest danger here is getting so caught up in your feelings that you talk for too long. Consider comfort levels and remember that your audience is bigger than just the person you are toasting, so it's best to save anything that should be said more privately for later.

> *Julie, you are my only sister, and I am so, so happy for you!*
> *You mean the world to me, and I am so pleased to know*
> *that you have found Mike, who is perfect for you. I love you*
> *very much, and wish you all the happiness you deserve!*

WHAT *NOT* TO SAY

Things to stay away from during a toast include

* Pointless stories (either cute or embarrassing) about the couple's childhoods—this is a wedding, not a roast. Make sure your anecdote is relevant to the occasion.

* Any mention of past loves. Period.

* References to any problems the couple may have had. This is *not* the time to bring up their two-month falling out over his Halloween costume.

* Talking about yourself instead of about them. This *is* the time to check your ego at the door.

WHEN *YOU* ARE THE ONE BEING TOASTED

What to do when you are the focus of all this praise? Easy—sit back (literally) and bask in the limelight. Even if others are standing, you should remain seated throughout the toast. Remember, too, not to drink when you're being toasted. Otherwise, it's like accepting any other compliment graciously: Keep your head up, don't be embarrassed, smile, and enjoy!

CHAMPAGNE TOASTS
Are You Ready?

Champagne is delightful—but not so delightful that it pours itself. Here are few tips to keep everyone's glasses full:

- First things first: Make sure everyone has something to toast with. If the toasts are during a cocktail party, signal the waitstaff to come around with more champagne shortly before you're ready to start. If you're at a seated dinner and you plan to have the toasts at the start of the evening, have glasses of champagne waiting at everyone's places or have them passed out as soon as everyone sits down. If you want to wait until a bit later, signal the waitstaff to have fresh glasses served or poured at the appropriate time.

- If you prefer not to use champagne, it's perfectly okay to toast using any beverage. Also, be sure to have a nonalcohol option such as sparkling cider or sparkling water for those who choose not to drink or for anyone underage.

- How many bottles will you need? Since the average champagne bottle pours about six glasses, divide your guest list by six to get the minimum number of bottles of champagne you should order.

Bottle — .75 liter, or six glasses

Magnum — 1.5 liters, or 12 glasses

Jeroboam — 3 liters, or 24 glasses

seven heavenly ways to fill a champagne glass

Champagne is so chic and classic that you can serve it on its own without a second thought. But since it's always fun to play dress-up, here are a few sophisticated alternatives that all use champagne as the base. For variety, try substituting an Italian Prosecco or Spanish Cava—both light, dry, sparkling wines—instead of champagne. And no matter which language you say *bubbly* in, just be sure it's served chilled!

name we know it by	to make: start with champagne and…	why it's so fabulous
MIMOSA	Add orange juice	Famous for making brunches divine
BELLINI	Add white peach juice or nectar	Chic Italian alternative to the mimosa
POM ROYALE	Add blueberry-pomegranate juice and fresh blueberries	Modern take on a classic Kir Royale—and a personal fave!
PIMM'S ROYALE	Add Pimm's	A refreshing twist on a very British summer staple
CHAMPS-ELYSÉES	Add Cointreau and triple sec or Cognac	Named for the elegant avenue in Paris, this is as sophisticated as it sounds.
CHAMPAGNE COCKTAIL	Add a bitters-soaked sugar cube (white or brown)	A classic. Dress this one—or any of these—up by rimming the glasses with a little colored sugar.
PASSION FRUIT CHAMPAGNE COCKTAIL	Add passion fruit juice or nectar	So exotic—not your garden-variety champagne! Even better, try adding star fruit (carambola) for a garnish; they're beautiful when sliced like a cucumber.

Adding strawberries, raspberries, blackberries, blueberries, or orange slices is a cheap and easy way to dress up straight champagne. Try placing a skewer of berries in the glass so guests can eat them without making a mess.

One for the History Books. One of the very best toasts I ever heard came from my cousin Nick, when he was best man at his brother Peter's wedding. Nick is a professional journalist, so he already has a leg up on the rest of us, but he really went above and beyond on this one. He spoke as though he were writing a letter to "Dear Abby," seeking advice on how to give a toast to a member of the Post family. He played on our family's relationship to Emily, poking gentle fun at etiquette and inserting little comments about Peter along the way. Emily would have loved it!

Emily Post

James Montgomery Flagg

EMILY POST, 1873 TO 1960

Emily Post began her career as a writer at the age of thirty-one. Her romantic stories of European and American society were serialized in *Vanity Fair*, *Collier's*, *McCall's*, and other popular magazines. Many were also successfully published in book form.

Upon its publication in 1922, her book, *Etiquette*, topped the nonfiction best-seller list, and the phrase "according to Emily Post" soon entered our language as the last word on the subject of social conduct. Mrs. Post, who as a girl had been told that well-bred women should not work, was suddenly a pioneering American woman. Her numerous books, a syndicated newspaper column, and a regular network radio program made Emily Post a figure of national stature and importance throughout the rest of her life.

"Good manners reflect something from inside—
an innate sense of consideration for others
and respect for self."

—Emily Post

also available *Emily Post's*

WEDDING ETIQUETTE

ISBN 978-0-06-074504-2 • Fifth Edition

wedding parties

ISBN 978-0-06-122801-8

*M*ake the wedding of your dreams a reality!

wedding planner for moms

ISBN 978-0-06-122800-1

wedding planner

ISBN 978-0-06-074503-5 • Fourth Edition

www.emilypost.com